A-Z NORWICH

CONTENTS

REFERENCE

A Road	A147
B Road	B1150
Dual Carriageway	
One-way Street Traffic flow on A roads is also indicated by a heavy line on the driver's left.	
Road Under Construction Opening dates are correct at the time of publication	
Proposed Road	
Restricted Access	
Pedestrianized Road	
Track / Footpath	
Residential Walkway	
Railway	Station / Heritage Station / Level Crossing
Built-up Area	CHURCH STREET
Local Authority Boundary	
Broads Authority Boundary	
Postcode Boundary	
Map Continuation	26 / Large Scale City Centre 5
Airport	

Car Park (selected)	P
Church or Chapel	†
City Wall (large scale only)	
Cycleway (selected)	
Fire Station	■
Hospital	H
House Numbers (A & B Roads only)	303 / 124
Information Centre	i
National Grid Reference	625
Park & Ride	Harford P+R
Police Station	▲
Post Office	★
Safety Camera with Speed Limit Fixed cameras and long term road works cameras Symbols do not indicate camera direction	30
Toilet: without facilities for the Disabled	▽
with facilities for the Disabled	▼
Educational Establishment	
Hospital or Healthcare Building	
Industrial Building	
Leisure or Recreational Facility	
Place of Interest	
Public Building	
Shopping Centre or Market	
Other Selected Buildings	

SCALE

Map Pages 6-42 1:15,840

0	¼	½ Mile
0	250	500	750 Metres

4 inches (10.16cm) to 1 mile   6.31cm to 1km

Map Pages 4-5 1:7,920

0	⅛	¼ Mile
0	100	200	300	400 Metres

8 inches (20.32cm) to 1 mile   12.63cm to 1km

Copyright of Geographers' A-Z Map Company Limited

Fairfield Road, Borough Green, Sevenoaks, Kent TN15 8PP
Tel: 01732 781000 (Enquiries & Trade Sales)
01732 783422 (Retail Sales)
www.az.co.uk
Copyright © Geographers' A-Z Map Co. Ltd.
EDITION 8 2013

C000172827

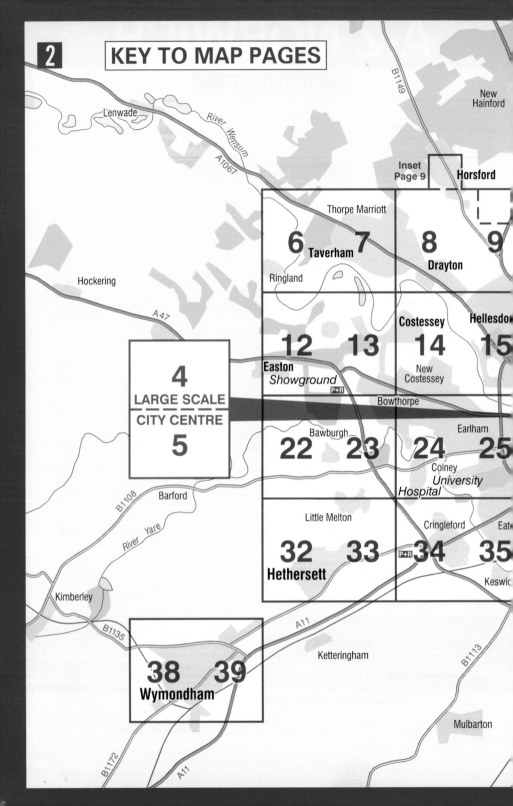

KEY TO MAP PAGES

2

New Hainford

Lenwade

River Wensum

A1067

B1149

Inset Page 9

Horsford

Thorpe Marriott

6 Taverham **7**

8 Drayton **9**

Ringland

Hockering

A47

Costessey

Hellesdon

12 **13**

14 **15**

Easton
Showground P+R
New Costessey

4
LARGE SCALE
CITY CENTRE
5

Bowthorpe

Bawburgh

Earlham

22 **23**

24 **25**

B1108
Barford

Colney
*University
Hospital*

River Yare

Little Melton

Cringleford

Eat

32 **33**

P+R **34** **35**

Hethersett

Keswic

Kimberley

B1135

A11

Ketteringham

B1113

38 **39**

Wymondham

Mulbarton

B1172

A11

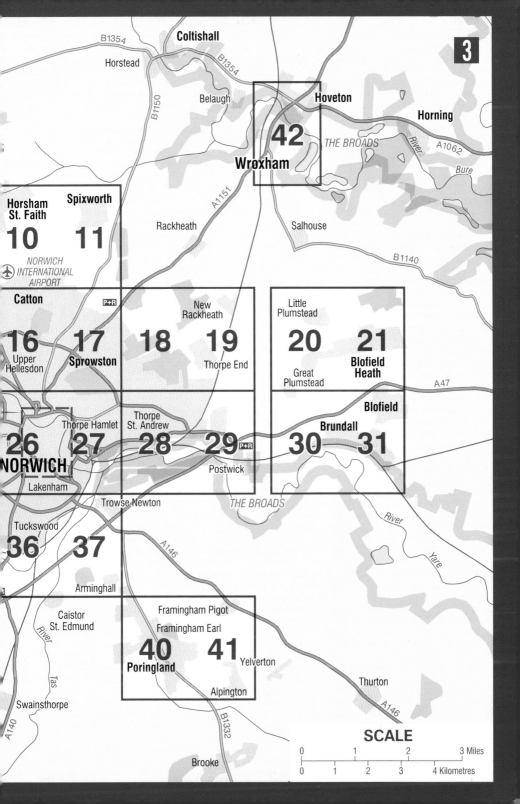

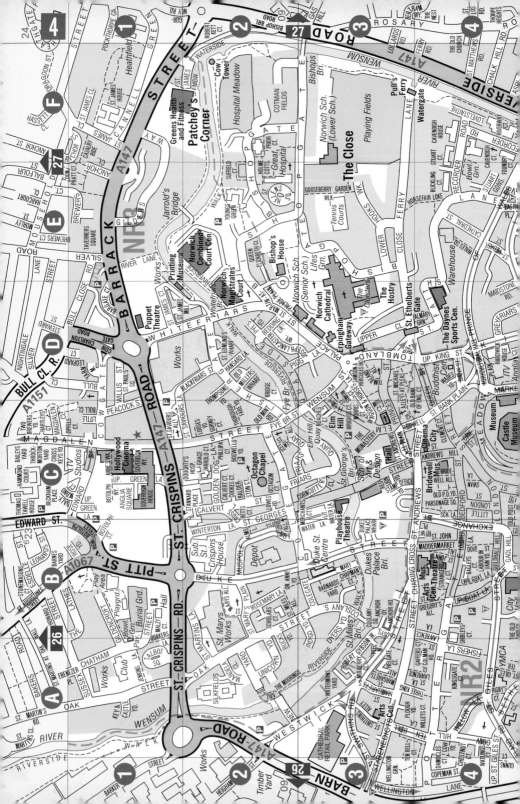

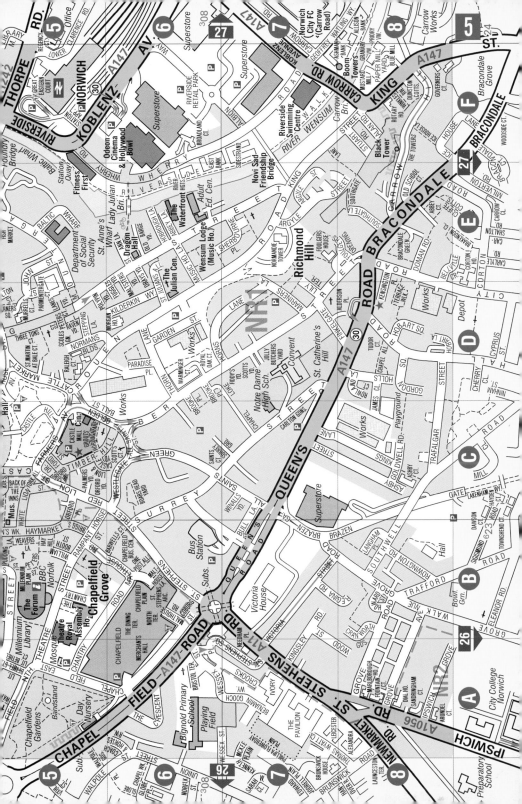

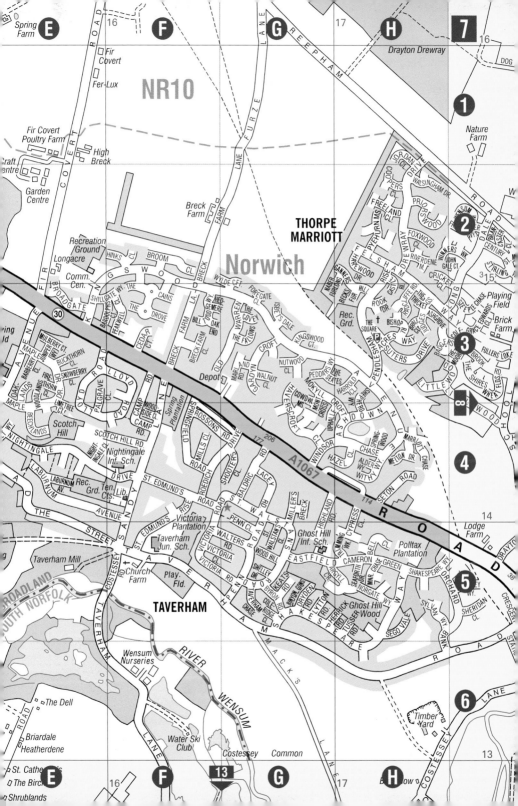

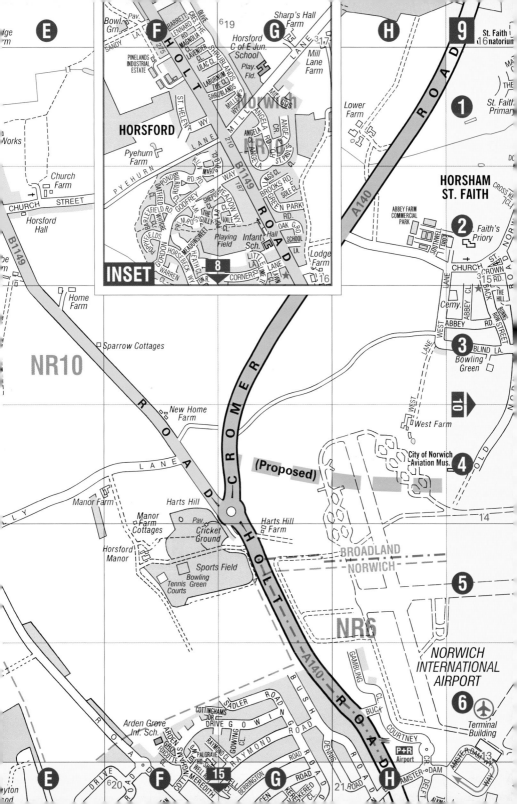

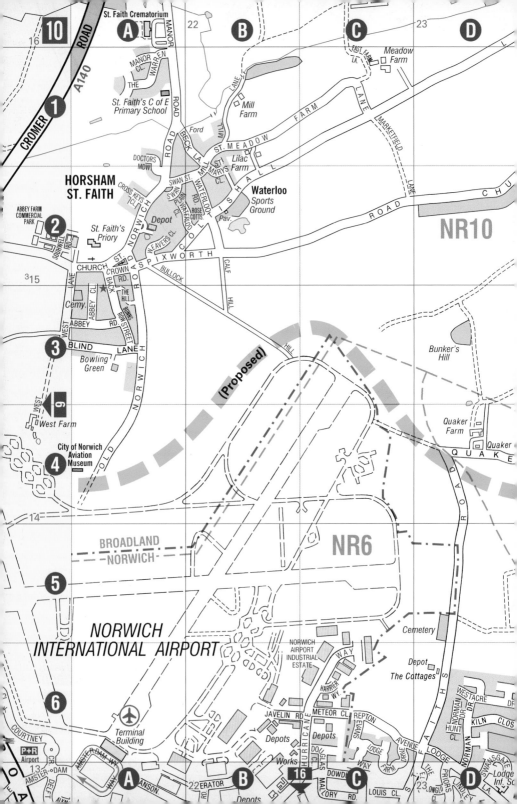

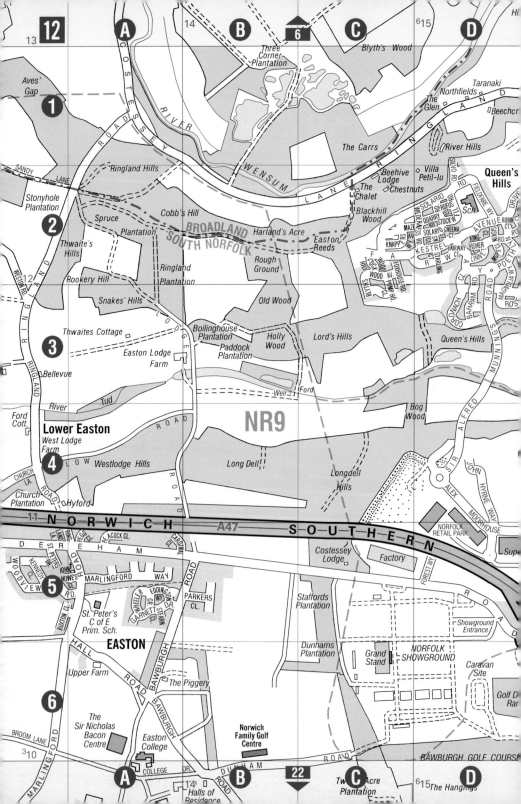

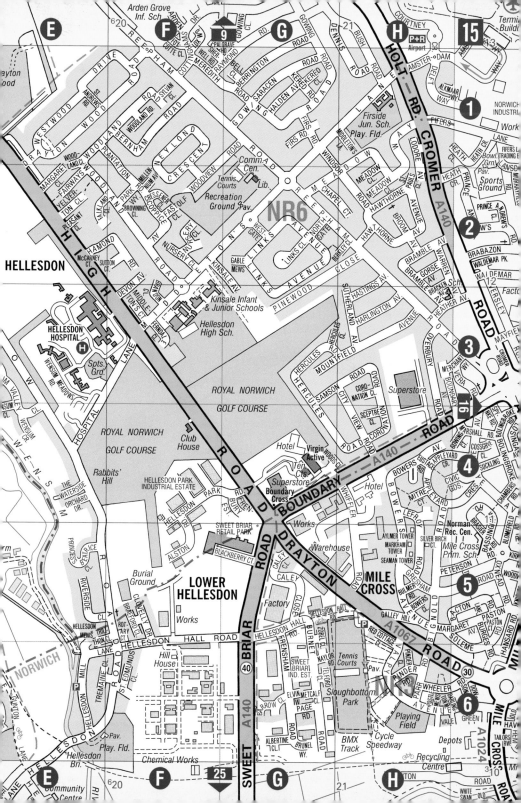

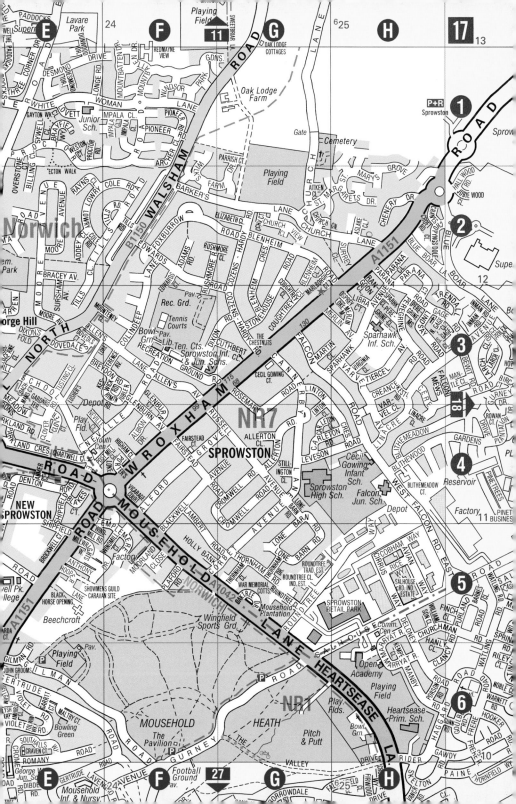

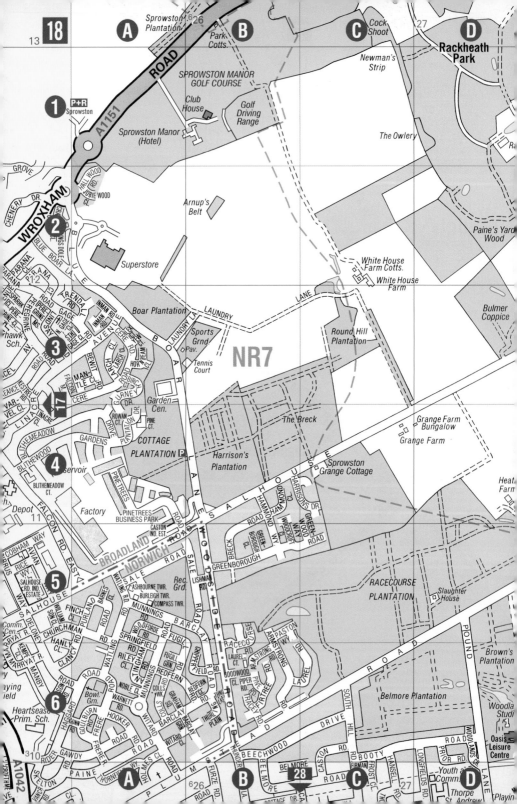

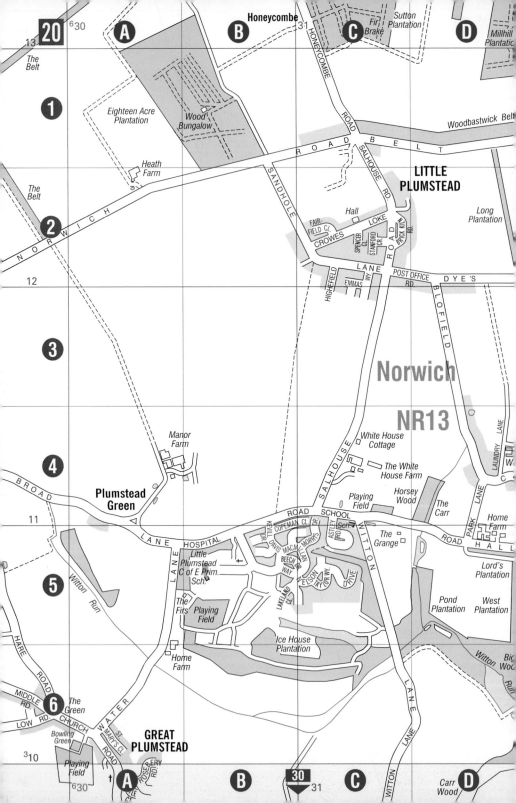

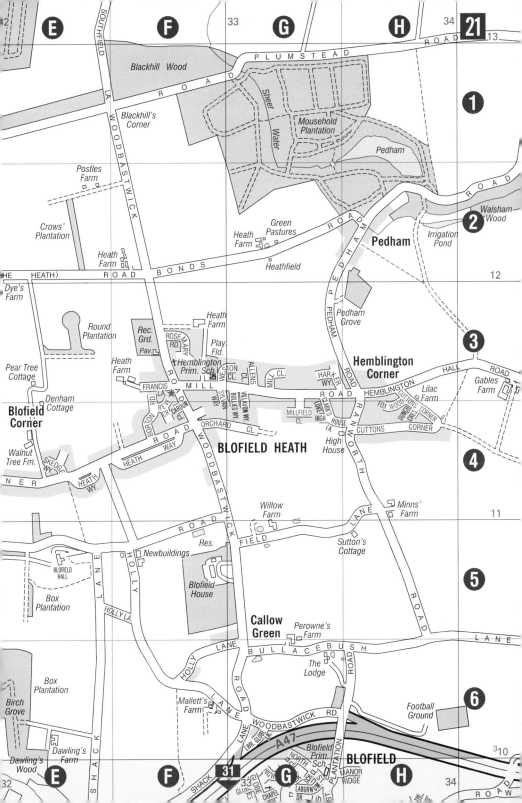

SOUTHFIELD LA.

PLUMSTEAD

ROAD

ROAD

Blackhill Wood

1

Blackhill's
Corner

Sheer
Water

Mousehold
Plantation

Pedham

WOODBASTWICK

Postles
Farm

ROAD

Walsham
Wood

Crows'
Plantation

Heath
Farm

Green
Pastures

Heath
Farm

2

Pedham

Irrigation
Pond

HE (HEATH) ROAD BONDS ROAD

Heathfield

PEDHAM

12

Dye's
Farm

Round
Plantation

Rec.
Grd.
Pav.

Heath
Farm

ROSE-
MARY
RD.

Play.
Fld.

Heath
Farm

Pedham
Grove

3

Pear Tree
Cottage

Heath
Farm

WESTON CL.

ALLENS CL.

Hemblington
Prim. Sch.

MILL CL.

HARKER
WY.

Hemblington
Corner

HALL

ROAD

Gables
Farm

Denham
Cottage

FRANCIS
LA.

MILL

SYLVAN
WAY

VILLANOW WY.

BULLIES WY.

HARKER
WY.

Lilac
Farm

CUTTONS

DUNCAN
CRES.

**Blofield
Corner**

BORTON
RD.

REV.
CR.

CARDUN
CL.

ORCHARD

CL.

MILLFIELD
CL.

HIGH

CLARK'S
HOUSE

HEMBLINGTON
ROAD

FOX
WOOD

CUTTONS
CORNER

ROAD

Walnut
Tree Fm.

SKEDGE
WY.

HEATH
WAY

WOODBASTWICK

BLOFIELD HEATH

LINKE
LA.

High
House

RANWORTH

4

NER

HEATH
WY.

ROAD

Willow
Farm

FIELD

LANE

Minns'
Farm

11

Sutton's
Cottage

ROAD

Res.

Newbuildings

5

BLOFIELD
HALL

HOLLY

Blofield
House

Box
Plantation

HOLLY LA.

**Callow
Green**

Perowne's
Farm

LANE

Box
Plantation

HOLLY

LANE

LANE

BULLACEBUSH

ROAD

The
Lodge

6

Football
Ground

Birch
Grove

Mallett's
Farm

ROAD

WOODBASTWICK RD.

Blofield
Prim.
Sch.

MANOR
RIDGE

BLOFIELD

3 10

Dawling's
Wood

Dawling's
Farm

SHACK

LANE

A47

LWR. GLOBE

NORTH

LABURNUM
DR.

CHAPEL

32 33

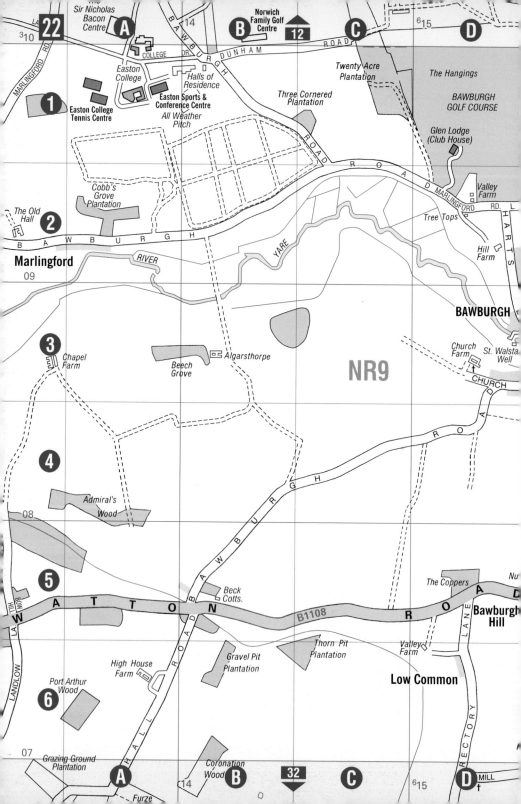

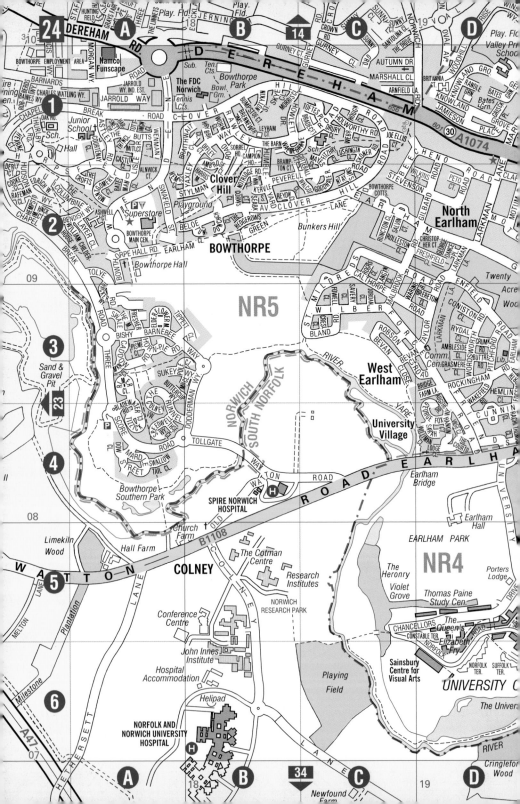

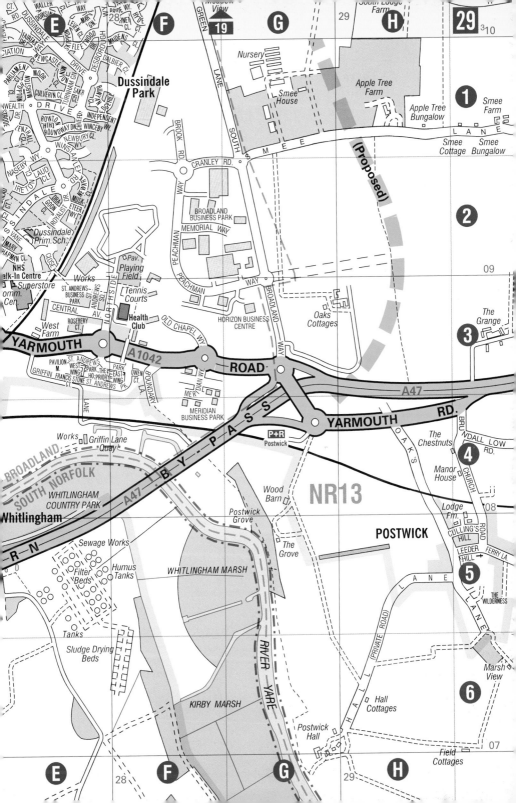

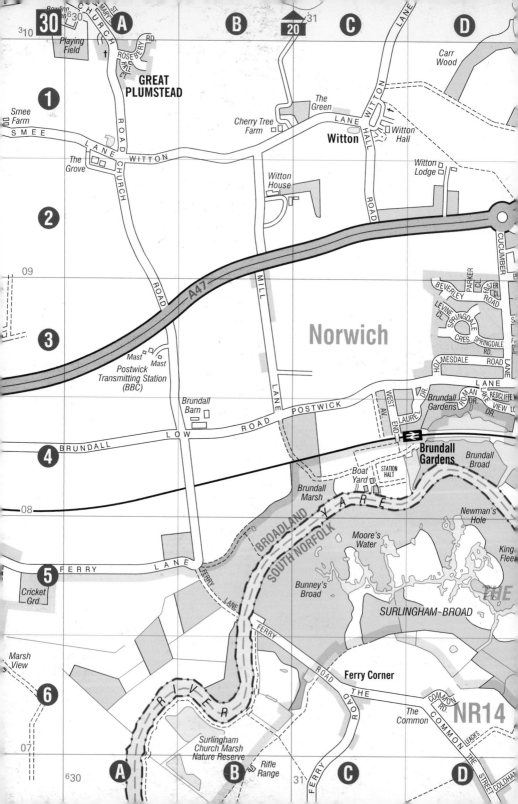

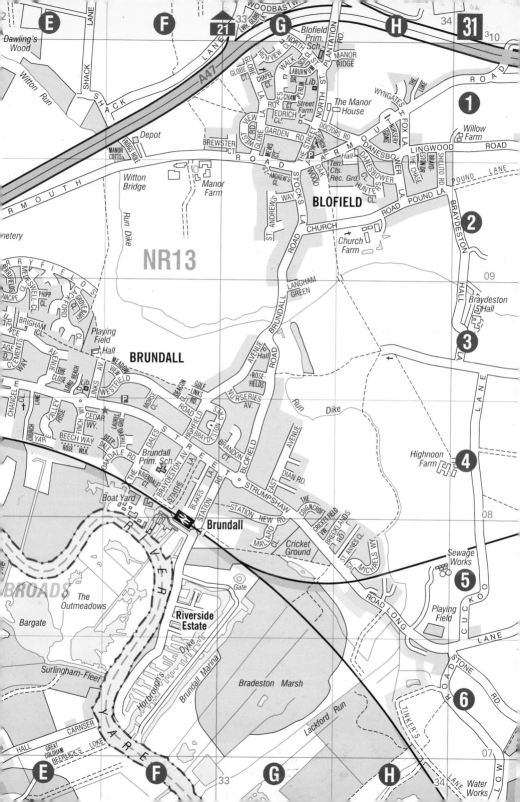

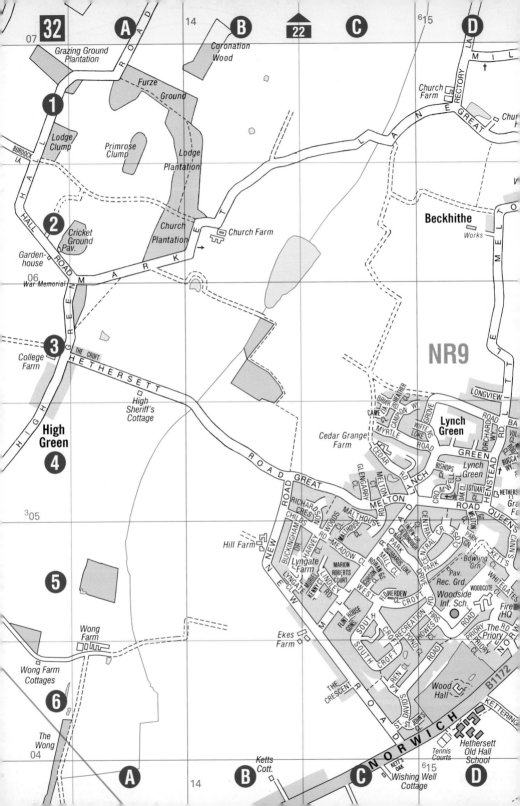

32

07

A 14 B C 615 D

22

Grazing Ground Plantation

Coronation Wood

Church Farm

❶ Furze Ground

BURDOCK LA.

Lodge Clump

Primrose Clump

Lodge Plantation

Garden-house

❷ Cricket Ground Pav.

Church Plantation

Church Farm

06 War Memorial

Beckhithe

Works

❸ THE CROFT

College Farm

HETHERSETT

High Sheriff's Cottage

NR9

LONGVIEW

305

High Green

❹

HIGH GREEN

Cedar Grange Farm

ROAD GREAT

CAMP

BRIAR RD

CAMPION WY

WIFFENS LOKE

MYRTLE ROAD

GROVE

CEDAR

Lynch Green

GREEN

ORCHARD WY

ROAD

BUCCA

BISHOPS CL

Lynch Green

WELL

CROI

OAK CL

STUART CL

HENSTEAD

PARK WY

HETHERS

Gra

GLENGARRY CL

MELTON CT

MELTON RD

MELTON ROAD

QUEEN'S

CANN'S

KETT'S

Hill Farm

RICHARDSON CRES.

CHILDS

BUCKINGHAM DR

HARVEY RD

WOODS RD

MALTHOUSE CL

MALTHOUSE CL

MEADOW CL

LINDLEY RD

MURIEL KENNICK CL

OAK

MILL

CENTRAL

CHUBARDS LOKE

PARK

CR

MELTON CLOSE

CENTRAL DRIVE

Bowling Grn.

WHITEGATES

WOODCOTE CL

Pav. Rec. Grd.

Woodside Inf. Sch.

Fire HQ

The Priory

PRIORY

❺

NEW ROAD

Lyngate Farm

LYNGATE RD

MARION ROBERTS COURT

ROWAN CL

FLOWERDEW CL

SOUTH CROFT

MILL CL

PRIORY CL

WEST

FLINT HOUSE GDNS.

RECREATION

HOWES CL

FIRS ROAD

POND CL

CROFT

Ekes Farm

Wong Farm

SOUTH CROFT

THE CRESCENT

ROAD

KEN CL

Wood Hall

B1172

KETTERING

❻

Wong Farm Cottages

MILL

ST. DAVIDS RD

ST. JOHN'S

Tennis Courts

Hethersett Old Hall School

The Wong

04

A 14 B Ketts Cott. C ❍NORWICH KETT'S OAK Wishing Well Cottage 615 D

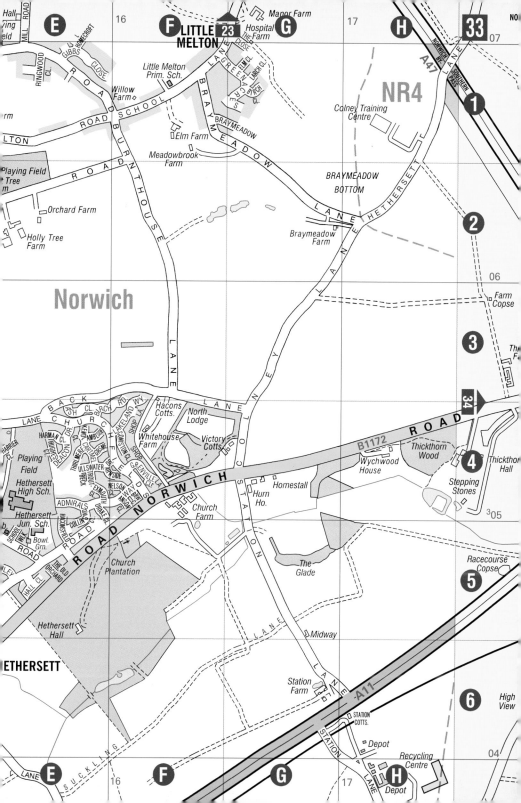

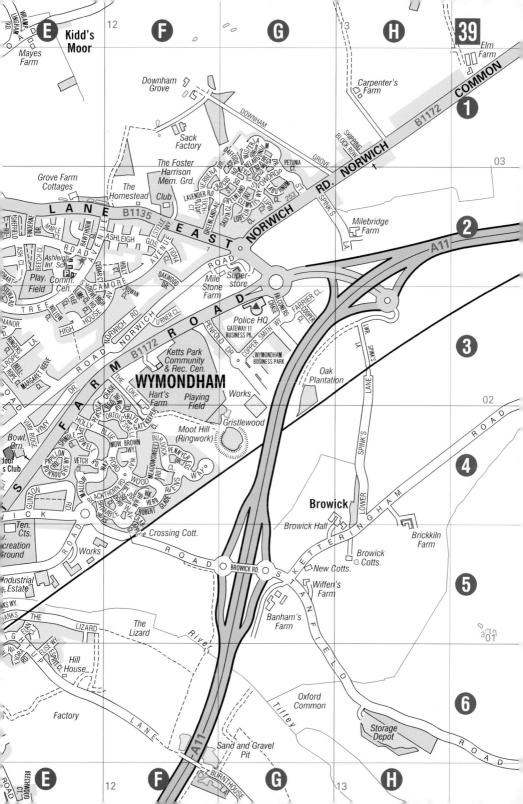

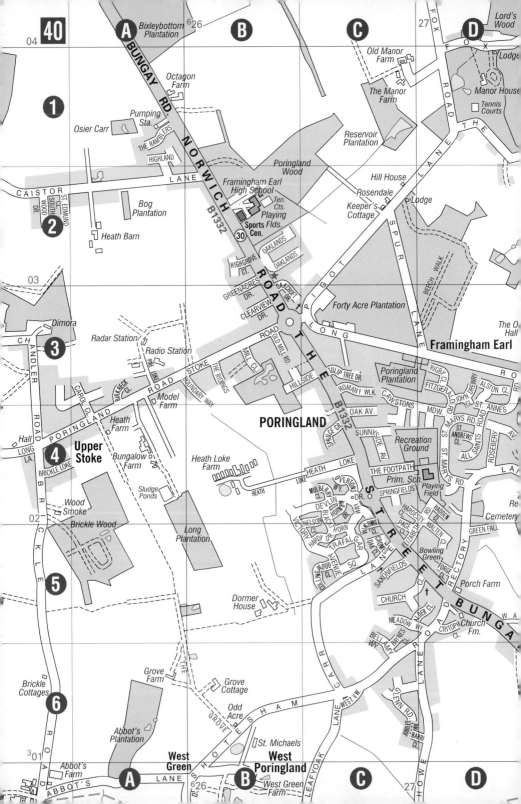

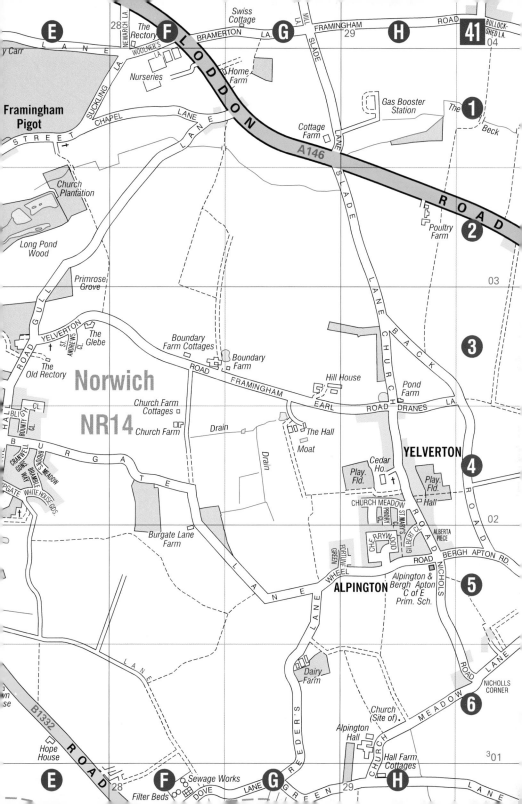

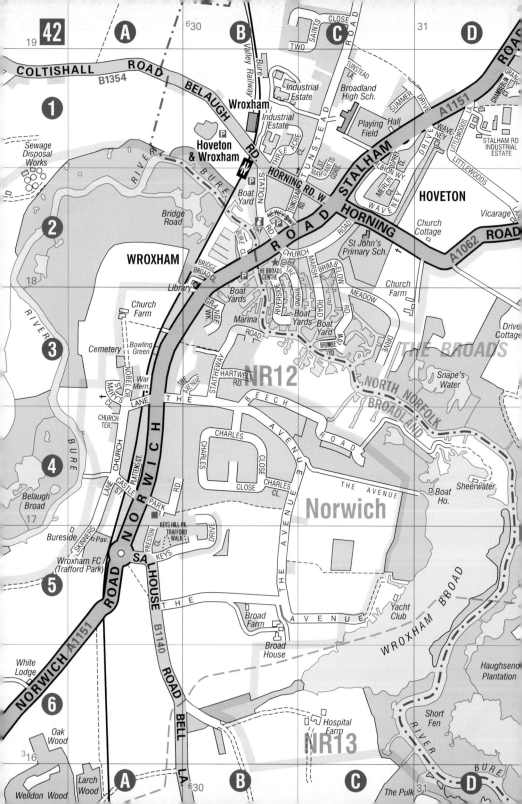

INDEX

Including Streets, Places & Areas, Hospitals etc., Industrial Estates,
Selected Flats & Walkways, Stations and Selected Places of Interest.

HOW TO USE THIS INDEX

1. Each street name is followed by its Postcode District, then by its Locality abbreviation(s) and then by its map reference;
   e.g. **Admirals Way** NR9: Hether . . . .4E **33** is in the NR9 Postcode District and the Hethersett Locality and is to be found in square 4E on page **33**. The page number is shown in bold type.

2. A strict alphabetical order is followed in which Av., Rd., St., etc. (though abbreviated) are read in full and as part of the street name;
   e.g. **Beechcroft** appears after **Beech Cl.** but before **Beech Dr.**

3. Streets and a selection of flats and walkways that cannot be shown on the mapping, appear in the index with the thoroughfare to which they are connected shown in brackets; e.g. **Barn Ter.** NR13: Brun . . . .3E **31** (off Long Reach)

4. Addresses that are in more than one part are referred to as not continuous.

5. Places and areas are shown in the index in BLUE TYPE and the map reference is to the actual map square in which the town centre or area is located and not to the place name shown on the map; e.g. BAWBURGH 3E 23

6. An example of a selected place of interest is City of Norwich Aviation Mus. 4A 10

7. An example of a station is **Brundall Gardens Station (Rail)** . . . .4D 30, also included is **Park & Ride**.
   e.g. **Airport (Park & Ride)** 6H 9

8. An example of a Hospital, Hospice or selected Healthcare facility is COLMAN HOSPITAL 5H 25

9. Map references for entries that appear on large scale pages **4** & **5** are shown first, with small scale map references shown in brackets;
   e.g. **Abbey Ct.** NR1: Norw 8E **5** (5E **27**)

GENERAL ABBREVIATIONS

All. : Alley	**Flds.** : Fields	**Nth.** : North
App. : Approach	**Gdn.** : Garden	**Pal.** : Palace
Arc. : Arcade	**Gdns.** : Gardens	**Pde.** : Parade
Av. : Avenue	**Ga.** : Gate	**Pk.** : Park
Bk. : Back	**Gt.** : Great	**Pl.** : Place
Bri. : Bridge	**Grn.** : Green	**Ri.** : Rise
Bldgs. : Buildings	**Gro.** : Grove	**Rd.** : Road
Bus. : Business	**Hgts.** : Heights	**Sth.** : South
Cen. : Centre	**Ho.** : House	**Sq.** : Square
Cl. : Close	**Ind.** : Industrial	**St.** : Street
Comn. : Common	**Info.** : Information	**Ter.** : Terrace
Cnr. : Corner	**La.** : Lane	**Twr.** : Tower
Cott. : Cottage	**Lit.** : Little	**Trad.** : Trading
Cotts. : Cottages	**Lwr.** : Lower	**Up.** : Upper
Ct. : Court	**Mnr.** : Manor	**Va.** : Vale
Cres. : Crescent	**Mkt.** : Market	**Vw.** : View
Cft. : Croft	**Mdw.** : Meadow	**Vis.** : Visitors
Dr. : Drive	**Mdws.** : Meadows	**Wlk.** : Walk
E. : East	**M.** : Mews	**W.** : West
Est. : Estate	**Mt.** : Mount	**Yd.** : Yard
Fld. : Field	**Mus.** : Museum	

LOCALITY ABBREVIATIONS

Alp : **Alpington**	Gt P : **Great Plumstead**	Rack : **Rackheath**
Arm : **Arminghall**	Helle : **Hellesdon**	R'land : **Ringland**
A'bridge : **Attlebridge**	Hemb : **Hemblington**	Sal : **Salhouse**
Baw : **Bawburgh**	Hether : **Hethersett**	Silf : **Silfield**
Bee A : **Beeston St Andrew**	H'ford : **Horsford**	Spix : **Spixworth**
Bel : **Belaugh**	Hor F : **Horsham St Faith**	Spro : **Sprowston**
Bix : **Bixley**	Hov : **Hoveton**	Stoke X : **Stoke Holy Cross**
Blof : **Blofield**	Howe : **Howe**	Stru : **Strumpshaw**
Bow : **Bowthorpe**	Int : **Intwood**	Surl : **Surlingham**
Bram : **Bramerton**	Kes : **Keswick**	Suton : **Suton**
Brun : **Brundall**	Kir B : **Kirby Bedon**	Swar : **Swardeston**
Caist E : **Caistor St Edmund**	Lit Mel : **Little Melton**	Tav : **Taverham**
Coln : **Colney**	Lit P : **Little Plumstead**	Thor E : **Thorpe End**
Cost : **Costessey**	Lwr H : **Lower Hellesdon**	Thor Mar : **Thorpe Marriott**
Cring : **Cringleford**	Mark : **Markshall**	Thor And : **Thorpe St Andrew**
Crost : **Crostwick**	Marl : **Marlingford**	Tro : **Trowse**
Dray : **Drayton**	New C : **New Costessey**	Wickle : **Wicklewood**
Eas : **Easton**	Norw : **Norwich**	Wit : **Witton**
Felth : **Felthorpe**	Old C : **Old Catton**	W'wick : **Woodbastwick**
Fram E : **Framingham Earl**	Panx : **Panxworth**	Wrox : **Wroxham**
Fram P : **Framingham Pigot**	Por : **Poringland**	Wym : **Wymondham**
Gt Mel : **Great Melton**	Post : **Postwick**	Yelv : **Yelverton**

A

	Abbot Rd. NR1: Norw 1C **36**
	Abbot's La. NR14: Por 6A **40**
	Aberdare Ct. NR1: Norw 2G **27**
Abbey Cl. NR10: Hor F 3A **10**	**Abinger Way**
Abbey Ct. NR1: Norw 8E **5** (5E **27**)	NR4: Norw 3H **35**
Abbey Farm Commercial Pk.	**Acacia Rd.** NR7: Thor And 1C **28**
NR10: Hor F 2H **9**	**Acland M.** NR6: Norw 3B **16**
Abbey La. NR1: Norw 6E **5** (4E **27**)	**Acorn Cl.** NR18: Wym 6D **38**
Abbey Rd. NR10: Hor F 3A **10**	**Acres Way** NR8: Thor Mar 3H **7**
NR18: Wym 6B **38**	**Adams Rd.** NR7: Spro 2F **17**
Abbot Cl. NR18: Wym 3D **38**	**Addey Cl.** NR6: Spro 2E **17**

Adelaide St. NR2: Norw 2A **26**
(not continuous)
Admirals Way NR9: Hether 4E **33**
Aerodrome Cres. NR7: Thor And 1A **28**
Aerodrome Rd. NR7: Thor And 1A **28**
Afghan Pl. NR3: Norw 6D **16**
Agricultural Hall Plain
NR1: Norw 4D **4** (3D **26**)
Airedale Cl. NR3: Norw 6B **16**
Airport (Park & Ride) 6H **9**
Aitken Cl. NR7: Spro 2G **17**

Brundall Gardens Station (Rail)—Church La.

Brundall Gardens Station (Rail) 4D 30
Brundall Low Rd. NR13: Post 4H 29 & 4A 30
Brundall Rd. NR13: Blof 3G 31
Brundall Station (Rail) 5F 31
Brunel Way NR3: Norw 6G 15
Brunswick Ho. NR2: Norw 7A 5
Brunswick Rd. NR2: Norw 7A 5 (5B 26)
Bryony Cl. NR6: Norw 2C 16
Buccaneer Way NR9: Hether 4D 32
Buck Courtney Cres. NR6: Norw 6H 9
Buckingham Dr. NR9: Hether 5B 32
Buckingham Rd. NR4: Norw 6G 25
Buckland Ri. NR4: Norw 3G 35
Bucks Yd. NR3: Norw 2A 4 (3C 26)
Buckthorn Cl. NR8: Tav 3E 7
Buck Yd. NR7: Thor And 4B 28
Bullacebush La. NR13: Blof 6G 21
Bullace Rd. NR5: New C 6A 14
Bullard Rd. NR3: Norw 4B 16
Bull Cl. NR3: Norw 1D 4 (2D 26)
Bull Cl. Rd. NR3: Norw 1D 4 (1D 26)
Bullies Way NR13: Blof 3G 21
Bull La. NR1: Norw 7B 5 (5D 26)
Bullock Hill NR10: Hor F 2A 10
Bullockshed La. NR14: Bram 1H 41
Bulmer Rd. NR3: Norw 5H 15
Bulrush Cl. NR10: H'ford 2F 9
Bumpstede Ct. NR5: Bow 1B 24
Bungalow La. NR7: Thor And 3D 28
Bungay Rd. NR14: Bix 3H 37 & 1A 40
NR14: Por 5D 40
Bunnett Sq. NR4: Norw 4G 25
Bunns Row NR10: Hor F 3A 10
Bunyan Cl. NR7: Thor And 1E 29
Burdock Cl. NR18: Wym 4F 39
Burdock La. NR9: Gt Mel 1A 32
Bure Cl. NR12: Wrox 2B 42
Bure Valley Railway
Wroxham Station 1B 42
Burgate La. NR14: Alp, Fram E, Por 4E 41
Burges Rd. NR3: Norw 5A 16
Burhill Cl. NR4: Norw 3H 35
Burleigh Twr. NR7: Norw 5A 18
Burma Rd. NR6: Old C 2E 17
Burnet Rd. NR3: Norw 5G 15
Burnthouse La. NR9: Hether, Lit Mel 1F 33
NR18: Silf 6G 39
Burroughs Way NR18: Wym 4E 39
Burton Cl. NR6: Norw 2B 16
Burton Dr. NR13: Rack 1G 19
Burton Rd. NR6: Norw 2B 16
Burton Rd. Bus. Pk. NR6: Norw 2B 16
Bury St. NR2: Norw 5A 26
Bush Rd. NR6: Helle 6G 9
Bussey Rd. NR6: Norw 3C 16
Buttercup Way NR5: Bow 3A 24
Buttermere Rd. NR5: Norw 3D 24
Butts, The NR5: Bow 1A 24
Buxton Cl. NR9: Eas 5A 12
Buxton Rd. NR3: Norw 1C 26
NR10: Spix 1F 11
NR12: Spix 6E 11
Byfield Ct. NR3: Norw 6B 16
Byron Rd. NR8: Tav 5G 7

C

Caddow Rd. NR5: Bow 3A 24
Cadge Cl. NR5: Norw 2E 25
Cadge M. NR5: Norw 3E 25
Cadge Rd. NR5: Norw 3E 25
(not continuous)
Caernarvon Rd. NR2: Norw 3A 26
Cains, The NR8: Thor Mar 3F 7
Cairns Ct. NR4: Norw 6A 26
Caistor La. NR14: Caist E, Por 6E 37 & 2A 40
CAISTOR ST EDMUND 6E 37
Caledonian Way NR6: Norw 3B 16
Caley Cl. NR3: Norw 5G 15
Calf Hill NR10: Hor F 2B 10
CALLOW GREEN 6G 21
Calthorpe Rd. NR5: Norw 2C 24
Calvert Ct. NR3: Norw 2C 4
Calvert St. NR3: Norw 2C 4 (2D 26)
Camberley Rd. NR4: Norw 1H 35
Camborne Cl. NR5: Norw 6D 14
Cambridge St. NR2: Norw 5B 26
Camelia Cl. NR9: Hether 4C 32
Cameron Grn. NR8: Tav 5H 7
Campbell Ct. NR3: Norw 1E 27
Camp Gro. NR1: Norw 3F 27
Campion Ho. NR5: Bow 1B 24
Campion Way NR9: Hether 4C 32
Camp Rd. NR8: Tav 4F 7
Canary Way NR1: Norw 5F 27
Canfor Rd. NR13: Rack 1G 19
Cannell Grn. NR3: Norw 1F 4 (2E 27)
Cannerby La. NR7: Spro 3G 17
Cann's La. NR9: Hether 5D 32
Canns Yd. *NR18: Wym 5D 38*
(off Brewery La.)
Canterbury Pl. NR2: Norw 2B 26
Cantley La. NR4: Cring 6A 34
(not continuous)
Capps Rd. NR3: Norw 6D 16
Cardiff Rd. NR2: Norw 4A 26
Cardigan Pl. NR2: Norw 2B 26
Cardinal Cl. NR9: Eas 5A 12
Cardun Cl. NR13: Blof 4F 21
Carleton Cl. NR7: Spro 4G 17
NR18: Wym 2D 38
Carleton Rd. NR7: Spro 4G 17
Carlton Gdns. NR1: Norw 7C 5
Carlyle Rd. NR1: Norw 8E 5 (6E 27)
Carnoustie NR4: Norw 2H 35
Carol Cl. NR14: Stoke X 3A 40
Caroline Ct. NR4: Norw 5G 25
Carpenters Ct. *NR4: Norw 5G 25*
(off Colman Rd.)
Carrefour Health & Beauty 4E 13
Carr La. NR14: Por 6C 40
Carrow Abbey 6F 27
Carrow Cl. NR1: Norw 8E 5
Carrow Hill NR1: Norw 8E 5 (5E 27)
Carrow Road 7F 5 (5F 27)
Carrow Rd. NR1: Norw 8F 5 (5E 27)
(not continuous)
Carr's Hill Cl. NR8: Cost 3B 14
Carshalton Rd. NR1: Norw 8E 5 (6E 27)
Carterford Dr. NR3: Norw 4D 16
Carter Rd. NR8: Dray 5C 8
Cartmel NR9: Hether 4E 33
Castle Hill NR1: Norw 5C 5 (4D 26)
Castle Mall NR1: Norw 5C 5 (4D 26)
Castle Mdw. NR1: Norw 5C 5 (4D 26)
Castle Museum & Art Gallery
Norwich 4C 4 (3D 26)
Castle Ri. NR8: Thor Mar 3H 7
Castle St. NR2: Norw 5C 5 (4D 26)
NR12: Wrox 4A 42
Castleton Cl. NR5: Bow 1A 24
Caston Ind. Est. NR7: Spro 5A 18
Caston Rd. NR7: Thor And 6C 18
Cathedral of St John the Baptist 3B 26
Cathedral Retail Pk. NR2: Norw 3A 4 (3B 26)
Cathedral St. NR1: Norw 4E 4 (3E 27)
Catherine Wheel Opening NR3: Norw 1C 26
Cator Rd. NR8: Dray 4A 8
Cattle Mkt. St. NR1: Norw 5D 5 (4D 26)
CATTON 2D 16
Catton Chase NR6: Old C 2C 16
Catton Ct. NR6: Old C 1D 16
Catton Gro. Rd. NR3: Norw 5C 16
NR6: Norw 4C 16
Catton Vw. Ct. NR3: Norw 4C 16
Causeway Cl. NR2: Norw 2B 26
Cavalier Cl. NR7: Thor And 2D 28
Cavalry Ride NR3: Norw 1F 4
Cavell Rd. NR1: Norw 1D 36
Cavendish Ct. NR1: Norw 4F 4
Cavendish Ho. NR1: Norw 4F 4 (3E 27)
Cavick Cotts. NR18: Wym 5B 38
Cavick Rd. NR18: Wym 5B 38
Cawstons Mdw. NR14: Por 3C 40
Cecil Gowing Ct. NR7: Spro 3G 17
Cecil Rd. NR1: Norw 6C 26
Cedar Av. NR10: Spix 1G 11
Cedar Ct. NR8: Tav 3F 7
NR18: Wym 2E 39
Cedar Rd. NR1: Norw 4F 27
NR9: Hether 4C 32
Cedars, The NR2: Norw 5A 26
Cedar Way NR13: Brun 4E 31
Cemetery La. NR18: Wym 5C 38
Central Av. NR7: Thor And 3E 29
Central Cl. NR9: Hether 5D 32
Central Cres. NR9: Hether 5D 32
Century Way NR8: Thor Mar 2A 8
Cere Rd. NR7: Spro 3H 17
Chalfont Wlk. NR4: Norw 1F 35
Chalgrove Fld. NR7: Thor And 1E 29
Chalk Hill Rd. NR1: Norw 4F 4 (3E 27)
Chamberlin Cl. NR3: Norw 5C 16
Chamberlin Ct. NR12: Hov 1D 42
NR13: Blof 1G 31
Chamberlin Rd. NR3: Norw 6C 16
Chambers Rd. NR3: Norw 4A 16
Chancel Cl. NR13: Brun 4E 31
Chancellors Dr. NR4: Norw 5C 24
Chandler Rd. NR14: Stoke X 3A 40
Chandler's Cl. NR18: Wym 5C 38
Chandlers Ct. NR4: Norw 3G 35
Chandler's Hill NR18: Wym 5C 38
Chantry, The NR2: Norw 5B 5 (4C 26)
Chantry Rd. NR2: Norw 5A 5 (4C 26)
Chapel All. NR1: Norw 8D 5
Chapel Break Rd. NR5: Bow 1H 23
Chapel Ct. NR6: Helle 2G 15
NR13: Blof 1G 31
Chapelfield NR2: Norw 6A 5 (4C 26)
Chapelfield Bus. Cen. NR2: Norw 6B 5
Chapel Fld. E. NR2: Norw 6A 5 (4C 26)
CHAPELFIELD GROVE 5B 5 (4C 26)
Chapel Fld. Nth. NR2: Norw 5A 5 (4C 26)
Chapelfield Plain NR2: Norw 6B 5
Chapel Fld. Rd. NR2: Norw 5A 5 (4B 26)
Chapel La. NR7: Thor And 3B 28
NR14: Fram P 1E 41
NR18: Wym 2A 38
Chapel Loke NR1: Norw 7C 5 (5D 26)
Chapel Rd. NR5: New C 5B 14
Chapel Wlk. NR2: Norw 6A 5
Chapel Yd. *NR10: Hor F 2A 10*
(off Church St.)
Chaplains Ho. *NR1: Norw 2E 4*
(off Bishopgate)
Charing Cross NR2: Norw 3B 4 (3C 26)
Charles Av. NR7: Thor And 2B 28
Charles Cl. NR12: Wrox 4B 42
Charles James Ct. *NR3: Norw 2C 4*
(off Fye Bri. St.)
Charles Jewson Ct. NR3: Norw 5A 16
Charles Sq. NR2: Norw 3B 26
Charles Watling Way NR5: Bow 1H 23
Charles Wesley Ct. *NR2: Norw 3A 26*
(off Belvoir St.)
Charlton Rd. NR3: Norw 1D 4 (2D 26)
Charolais Cl. NR14: Tro 1G 37
Chartwell Ct. NR7: Spro 4E 17
Chartwell Rd. NR6: Norw 4C 16
NR7: Norw 4C 16
Chase, The NR13: Blof 2H 31
Chase Cl. NR6: Old C 2C 16
Chatham St. NR3: Norw 1A 4 (2C 26)
Cheena Ct. NR8: Cost 2D 12
Chenery Dr. NR7: Spro 2H 17
Cherry Cl. NR1: Norw 8D 5 (6D 26)
Cherrywood NR14: Alp 5H 41
Chester Pl. NR2: Norw 4B 26
Chester St. NR2: Norw 5B 26
Chestnut Av. NR10: Spix 1G 11
Chestnut Cl. NR5: New C 5H 13
Chestnut Ct. NR2: Norw 4A 4
Chestnut Dr. NR18: Wym 6B 38
Chestnut Hill NR4: Norw 2F 35
Chestnuts, The NR7: Spro 3G 17
NR18: Wym 3C 38
Cheyham Mt. NR4: Norw 2G 35
Childs Rd. NR9: Hether 4B 32
Childs Ter. NR9: Baw 3E 23
Chipperfield Rd. NR7: Norw 6B 18
Chittock Cl. NR10: Spix 3G 11
Chopyngs Dole Cl. NR7: Spro 2H 17
Choseley Ct. NR18: Wym 4D 38
Christchurch Rd. NR2: Norw 4H 25
Christine Rd. NR10: Spix 3G 11
Christopher Cl. NR1: Norw 1C 36
Christopher Ct. NR5: Norw 2D 24
Church All. NR2: Norw 3C 4
NR13: Blof 1G 31
Church Av. NR2: Norw 6A 26
Church Av. E. NR2: Norw 6A 26
Church Cl. NR2: Norw 1A 26
NR14: Arm 6H 37
NR14: Por 5C 40
Churchfield NR4: Cring 3E 35
Churchfield Grn. NR7: Thor And 1A 28
Churchfields NR9: Hether 4E 33
Church Grn. NR7: Spro 2G 17
Churchill Rd. NR3: Norw 1D 26
Church La. NR4: Norw 2F 35
NR7: Spro 2G 17
NR9: Eas 4A 12
NR10: Spix 2D 10
NR12: Bee A 2G 17

46 A-Z Norwich

De Caux Rd.—Fastolf Cl.

De Caux Rd. NR3: Norw 6D 16
Deepdale NR13: Brun 4F 31
Deep Rd. NR18: Wym 1C 38
Defiant Rd. NR6: Norw 2C 16
De Hague Rd. NR4: Norw 5G 25
Delane Rd. NR8: Dray 6D 8
Delft Way NR6: Norw 1H 15
Dell, The NR14: Tro 1G 37
Dell Cres. NR5: Norw 2F 25
Dell Loke NR14: Tro 1G 37
Dell Rose Ct. NR4: Norw 5F 25
Deloney Rd. NR7: Norw 5H 17
Delta Cl. NR6: Norw 3B 16
Denbigh Ho. NR2: Norw 3A 26
Denbigh Rd. NR2: Norw 4A 26
Denes, The NR7: Thor And 4H 27
Denmark Opening NR3: Norw 6D 16
Denmark Rd. NR3: Norw 6D 16
Denmead Cl. NR4: Norw 3H 35
Dennis Rd. NR6: Helle 6G 9
Denton Rd. NR3: Norw 4E 17
Derby St. NR2: Norw 2B 26
Dereham Rd. NR2: Norw 2G 25
NR5: Bow, New C 5E 13
(not continuous)
NR9: Eas, New C 5A 12
Dersley Ct. NR5: Bow 2H 23
Desborough Way NR7: Thor And 1E 29
Desmond Dr. NR6: Old C 1E 17
Devlin Dr. NR14: Por 4C 40
Devon Av. NR6: Helle 3F 15
Devonshire Pl. *NR2: Norw 2B 26*
(off Devonshire St.)
Devonshire St. NR2: Norw 2A 26
Devon Way NR14: Tro 1H 37
Dial Ho. NR2: Norw 8A 5
Diamond Rd. NR6: Norw 2A 16
Dian Rd. NR13: Brun 4G 31
Dibden Rd. NR3: Norw 1E 27
Dining Terrace, The NR2: Norw 6B 5
Distillery Sq. NR2: Norw 3B 26
Dixon Rd. NR7: Spro 3F 17
Dixons Fold NR6: Old C 3E 17
Doctors Mdw. NR10: Hor F 1A 10
Doctors Rd. NR13: Blof 1G 31
Dodderman Way NR5: Bow 4B 24
Dog La. NR10: H'ford 1A 8
Dogwood Cl. NR18: Wym 4F 39
Dogwood Rd. NR6: Norw 3C 16
Dolphin Gro. NR2: Norw 1A 26
Dolphin Path NR2: Norw 1A 26
Dolphin Rd. NR5: New C 6F 13
Doman Rd. NR1: Norw 8E 5 (5E 27)
Donchurch Cl. NR5: Bow 2B 24
Donkey La. NR4: Norw 2G 35
Don Pratt Ct. NR3: Norw 1E 4
Doris Rd. NR2: Norw 4A 26
Doughty's Hospital NR3: Norw 2C 4
Douglas Cl. NR6: Norw 6C 10
Douglas Haig Rd. NR5: Norw 3E 25
Douglas Rd. NR10: Spix 3F 11
Douro Pl. NR2: Norw 3B 26
Dovedales NR6: Spro 3E 17
Dovedales Ct. NR6: Spro 3E 17
Dove La. NR14: Howe 6F 41
Dover St. NR2: Norw 4A 26
Dove St. NR2: Norw 4B 4
Dow Cl. NR5: Bow 4A 24
Dowding Rd. NR6: Norw 1C 16
DOWNHAM 1D 38
Downham Cres. NR18: Wym 2D 38
Downham Gro. NR18: Wym 1G 39
Downing M. NR5: Bow 1G 23
Dowsing Ct. NR7: Thor And 6E 19
Dowson Rd. NR3: Norw 6A 16
Dragonfly La. NR4: Cring 3C 34
Dragon Hall 6E 5 (4E 27)
Dragoon Cl. NR7: Thor And 2E 29
Dragoon St. NR3: Norw 1F 4 (1E 27)
Drake Cl. NR9: Hether 4E 33
Dranes La. NR14: Yelv 4H 41
Draper Way NR5: Bow 1G 23
Drays Yd. NR1: Norw 6E 5 (4E 27)
DRAYTON 5B 8
Drayton Gro. NR8: Dray 5A 8
Drayton Hall Pk. NR8: Dray 5C 8
Drayton Hall Pk. Rd. NR8: Dray 5C 8
Drayton High Rd. NR6: Helle 5B 8
NR8: Dray 5B 8
Drayton Ind. Est. NR8: Dray 5A 8
Drayton La. NR10: H'ford 3D 8
Drayton Lodge Pk. NR8: Dray 6C 8
Drayton Rd. NR3: Norw 5G 15
Drayton Wood Rd. NR6: Helle 1E 15
Drewray Dr. NR8: Thor Mar 2H 7
Drive, The NR5: New C 1C 24
NR14: Bix 1H 37
Drove, The NR8: Thor Mar 3F 7
Dr Torrens Way NR5: New C 6G 13
Drury Cl. NR5: Bow 1C 24
Dryden Rd. NR8: Tav 5G 7
Duckett Cl. NR1: Norw 2D 36
Duff Rd. NR3: Norw 5C 16
Dugard Av. NR1: Norw 1G 27
Dukes Pal. Wharf NR3: Norw 3B 4
Duke St. NR3: Norw 2B 4 (2C 26)
Dunch Cres. NR13: Hemb 4H 21
Dunham Rd. NR9: Eas 1B 22
Dunnock Ct. *NR8: Cost 2E 13*
(off Dunnock Dr.)
Dunnock Dr. NR8: Cost 2D 12
Dunston Cotts. NR1: Norw 8F 5
Dunwood Dr. NR6: Old C 6E 11
Durham St. NR2: Norw 5A 26
Dussindale NR18: Wym 2D 38
Dussindale Dr. NR7: Thor And 5E 19
(not continuous)
DUSSINDALE PARK 1E 29
Duverlin Cl. NR4: Norw 2H 35
Dyers Yd. NR3: Norw 3B 4 (3C 26)
Dye's Rd. NR13: Blof 2D 20
Dykebeck NR18: Wickle, Wym 5A 38

E

Eade Rd. NR3: Norw 1C 26
Eagle Wlk. NR2: Norw 5B 26
Earles Gdns. NR4: Norw 4F 25
EARLHAM 4E 25
Earlham Ct. NR2: Norw 3B 26
Earlham Crematorium NR2: Norw 3H 25
Earlham Five Ways NR4: Norw 4E 25
Earlham Grn. La. NR4: Norw 2C 24
NR5: Bow, Norw 2A 24
Earlham Gro. NR5: Norw 3E 25
Earlham Ho. NR2: Norw 4H 25
Earlham Ho. Shops *NR2: Norw 4H 25*
(off Earlham Rd.)
EARLHAM RISE 3F 25
Earlham Rd. NR2: Norw 3G 25
NR4: Norw 4D 24
Earlham W. Cen. NR5: Norw 3D 24
Earnshaw Ct. NR7: Thor And 3B 28
East Av. NR13: Brun 4G 31
East Bank NR1: Norw 6F 5
Eastbourne Pl. NR1: Norw 4E 4 (3E 27)
Eastern Av. NR7: Thor And 2D 28
Eastern Cl. NR7: Thor And 2D 28
Eastern Cres. NR7: Thor And 2D 28
Eastern Rd. NR7: Thor And 2D 28
East Farm La. NR10: Hor F 1C 10
Eastfield NR8: Tav 5G 7
East Hills Rd. NR5: New C 6G 13
Eastlodge NR1: Norw 3H 27
EASTON 5A 12
Easton College Tennis Cen. 1A 22
Easton Sports & Conference Cen. 1A 22
East Wing NR7: Thor And 3F 29
Eastwood M. NR6: Old C 4D 16
EATON 2F 35
Eaton Cen. NR4: Norw 2F 35
Eaton Chase NR4: Norw 1F 35
Eaton Gate NR4: Kes 5G 35
Eaton Golf Course 2H 35
Eaton Rd. NR4: Norw 1A 36
Eaton St. NR4: Norw 3E 35
Eaton Vale Activity Cen. 4G 35
Ebbisham Dr. NR4: Norw 3G 35
Ebenezer Pl. NR3: Norw 1A 4 (1C 26)
Ecton Wlk. NR6: Old C 2E 17
Eddington Way NR9: Eas 5A 12
Eden Cl. NR7: Norw 3H 27
Edenhurst Cl. NR4: Norw 6G 25
Edgefield Cl. NR6: Old C 6E 11
Edgehill NR7: Thor And 1E 29
Edgeworth Rd. NR5: Norw 3D 24
Edinburgh Rd. NR2: Norw 3H 25
Edmund Bacon Ct. NR3: Norw 6C 16
Edrich Cl. NR13: Blof 1G 31
Edrich Way NR5: Bow 2H 23
Edward Gambling Ct. NR2: Norw 1A 26
Edward Jodrell Plain NR2: Norw 7A 5 (5B 26)
Edwards Ct. NR7: Spro 2F 17
Edwards Rd. NR7: Spro 2F 17
Edward St. NR3: Norw 1B 4 (1D 26)
Edwin Cl. NR18: Wym 3C 38
Elan Cl. NR18: Wym 5E 39
Elder Cl. NR5: New C 5C 14
Elderflower M. NR5: Bow 3A 24
Eleanor Rd. NR1: Norw 8B 5 (6C 26)
Elise Way NR18: Wym 6E 39
Elizabeth Av. NR7: Thor And 2C 28
Elizabeth Cl. NR7: Spro 2G 17
NR10: Spix 1F 11
Elizabeth Fry Rd. NR2: Norw 4G 25
Elizabeth Rd. NR14: Por 5C 40
Elkins Rd. NR18: Wym 3C 38
Ella Rd. NR1: Norw 3F 27
Ellcar Ri. NR4: Norw 2H 35
Ellis Gdns. NR4: Kes 6G 35
Elm Cl. NR5: New C 5A 14
NR9: Lit Mel 1G 33
Elmdon Ct. NR1: Norw 3F 27
Elm Gro. La. NR3: Norw 5C 16
Elm Hill 3C 4
Elm Hill NR3: Norw 3C 4 (3D 26)
Elms, The NR2: Norw 4A 26
NR6: Old C 1D 16
Elm Ter. NR18: Wym 4D 38
Elstead Cl. NR4: Norw 3G 35
Elveden Cl. NR4: Norw 2G 35
Elvina Rd. NR10: Spix 2F 11
Elvin Way NR3: Norw 6G 15
Elwyn Rd. NR1: Norw 1D 36
Ely St. NR2: Norw 2B 26
Embry Cres. NR6: Norw 1C 16
Emmas Way NR13: Lit P 2C 20
Enfield Rd. NR5: Norw 3D 24
English Rd. NR6: Old C 3D 16
Erins, The NR3: Norw 6D 16
Ernest Gage Av. NR5: New C 5E 13
Erpingham Gateway 3D 4
Esdelle St. NR3: Norw 1B 4 (1C 26)
Esprit Cl. NR18: Wym 6E 39
Essex St. NR2: Norw 4B 26
Estelle Way NR18: Wym 2F 39
Ethel Gooch Rd. NR18: Wym 3C 38
Ethel Rd. NR1: Norw 4F 27
Europa Way NR1: Norw 1F 37
Europa Way Ind. Est.
NR1: Norw 1F 37
Eustace Rd. NR3: Norw 4H 15
Evans Way NR6: Old C 6C 10
Eva Rd. NR13: Rack 1G 19
Eversley Rd. NR6: Helle 3A 16
Everson Cl. NR5: New C 6D 14
Evora Rd. NR18: Wym 6E 39
Exchange St. NR2: Norw 4B 4 (3C 26)
Exeter St. NR2: Norw 2B 26
Exige Way NR18: Wym 6E 39
Exmouth Cl. NR9: Hether 4E 33

F

Fairfax Dr. NR7: Thor And 6E 19
Fairfax Rd. NR4: Norw 5G 25
Fairfield Cl. NR13: Lit P 2C 20
Fairfield Rd. NR2: Norw 6B 26
Fairhaven Ct. NR2: Norw 3H 25
Fairland Ct. *NR18: Wym 5D 38*
(off Fairland St.)
Fairland St. NR18: Wym 5D 38
Fairmile Cl. NR2: Norw 6A 26
Fairstead Ct. NR7: Spro 4F 17
Fairstead Rd. NR7: Spro 4F 17
Fairview Cl. NR8: Dray 6B 8
Fairway NR8: Cost 2C 12
Fairway Ct. NR8: Cost 2D 12
Fairways NR6: Helle 2E 15
Fakenham Rd. NR8: Dray, Tav 1A 6
NR9: A'bridge 1A 6
Falconers Chase NR18: Wym 3G 39
Falcon M. NR7: Spro 3H 17
Falcon Rd. E. NR7: Spro 4H 17
Falcon Rd. W. NR7: Spro 3G 17
Falkland Cl. NR6: Helle 2E 15
Fallowfield NR14: Fram E, Por 4D 40
Fallowfield Cl. NR1: Norw 1H 27
Fallows, The NR8: Thor Mar 3G 7
Farmers Av. NR1: Norw 5C 5 (4D 26)
Farmland Rd. NR5: New C 5A 14
Farrier Cl. NR18: Wym 3G 39
Farrow Rd. NR5: Norw 3G 25
Fastolf Cl. NR6: Helle 2F 15

G

Laburnum Dr.—Mancroft St.

Laburnum Dr. NR13: Blof 1G 31
Lacey Rd. NR8: Tav 4G 7
Lackford Cl. NR13: Brun 3E 31
Ladbrooke Pl. NR1: Norw 2F 27
Lady Betty Rd. NR1: Norw 6C 26
Lady Mary Rd. NR1: Norw 6C 26
Lady's La. NR18: Wym 5B 38
Ladysmith Rd. NR3: Norw 6E 17
Lakeland Cl. NR13: Lit P 5B 20
Lakeland Way NR9: Hether 4F 33
Lakenfields NR1: Norw 1E 37
LAKENHAM 6D 26
Lakenham Rd. NR4: Norw 1B 36
Lakenham Way NR1: Norw 8C 5 (6D 26)
NR4: Norw 2D 36
Lake Vw. Dr. NR13: Brun 3D 30
Lambert Ho. *NR5: Bow 1B 24*
(off Humbleyard)
Lambert Rd. NR7: Spro 4F 17
Lancaster Cl. NR6: Old C 1C 16
Lanchester Ct. NR2: Norw 2A 26
Landlow La. NR9: Gt Mel 6A 22
Lane, The NR3: Norw 5A 16
Lanes Yd. NR1: Norw 5D 5
Langham Grn. NR13: Blof 3G 31
Langham Pl. NR1: Norw 8B 5 (5C 26)
Langley Cl. NR4: Cring 4D 34
Langley Wlk. NR2: Norw 2A 26
Langton Cl. NR5: Norw 2C 24
Lansdowne Rd. NR6: Norw 1A 16
Lapwing Dr. NR8: Cost 2E 13
Larch Cl. NR7: Spro 3A 18
NR9: Lit Mel 1G 33
Larkman La. NR5: Norw 3D 24
Larkman Rd. NR5: Norw 2D 24
Larners Way *NR3: Norw 6H 15*
(off Wheeler Rd.)
Lathes, The NR3: Norw 1B 4 (2C 26)
Latimer Rd. NR1: Norw 1D 36
Laud Cl. NR7: Thor And 2E 29
Launceston Ter. NR2: Norw 8A 5
Laundry Cl. NR7: Thor And 2B 28
Laundry La. NR7: Spro 3A 18
NR7: Thor And 2C 28
NR13: Blof 4D 20
Laurel Ct. NR7: Thor And 6B 18
Laurel Dr. NR13: Brun 4C 30
Laurel Gro. NR13: Brun 4F 31
Laurel Rd. NR7: Thor And 6C 18
Lavare Ct. NR6: Old C 1D 16
Lavender Cl. NR10: H'ford 1F 9
Lavender Rd. NR18: Wym 2F 39
Lavengro Rd. NR3: Norw 1E 27
Lawn Cl. NR10: H'ford 2G 9
Lawn Cres. NR13: Thor E 4F 19
Lawson Rd. NR3: Norw 6D 16
Layer Cl. NR5: Bow 2A 24
Layson Dr. NR3: Norw 6D 16
Layton Cl. NR8: Dray 6C 8
Leach's Turn NR14: Surl 6D 30
Leafyoak La. NR14: Por 6C 40
Leas Ct. NR6: Norw 1E 25
Leeder Hill NR13: Post 5H 29
Leewood Cres. NR5: Norw 6D 14
Lefroy Rd. NR3: Norw 4H 15
Legarda Ct. NR3: Norw 5E 17
Leicester NR2: Norw 7A 5
Leicester St. NR2: Norw 5B 26
Lemon Av. NR2: Norw 3G 25
Leng Cres. NR4: Norw 1F 35
Lenthall Cl. NR7: Thor And 1E 29
Leonards St. NR3: Norw 1B 4 (1C 26)
Leopard Ct. NR3: Norw 1D 4 (2D 26)
Leopold Cl. NR4: Norw 6H 25
Leopold Rd. NR4: Norw 6H 25
Le Strange Cl. NR2: Norw 4G 25
Le Tunder Cl. NR7: Thor And 2B 28
Leven Cl. NR7: Thor And 6E 19
Leveson Rd. NR7: Spro 4G 17
Levine Cl. NR13: Brun 3D 30
Leyham Ct. NR5: Bow 1B 24
Liberator Rd. NR6: Norw 1B 16
Libra Ct. NR7: Spro 3H 17
Lilac Cl. NR10: H'ford 1F 9
Lilburne Av. NR3: Norw 5C 16
Lilian Cl. NR6: Helle 3A 16
Lilian Rd. NR10: Spix 1F 11
Lilly Ter. NR1: Norw 7D 5 (5D 26)
Lime Kiln M. NR3: Norw 1B 26
Lime Tree Av. NR7: Thor And 2H 27
NR8: Cost 3A 14
NR18: Wym 2D 38
Lime Tree Cl. NR10: H'ford 2G 9
NR18: Wym 3E 39
Limetree Ct. NR8: Tav 4E 7
Lime Tree Rd. NR2: Norw 6A 26
Linacre Av. NR7: Spro 4H 17
Linacre Cl. NR7: Spro 4H 17
Linalls Dr. NR8: Cost 3F 13
Lincoln St. NR2: Norw 4A 26
Linden Dr. NR9: Hether 5C 32
Linden Rd. NR5: New C 6D 14
Lindford Dr. NR4: Norw 3G 35
Lindley Cl. NR6: Old C 1D 16
Lindley Rd. NR9: Hether 5C 32
Lindley St. NR1: Norw 6D 26
Lindsay Rd. NR7: Spro 3H 17
Lings Cl. NR10: H'ford 2G 9
Lingwood Rd. NR13: Blof 1H 31
Links Av. NR6: Helle 2G 15
NR13: Brun 3E 31
Links Cl. NR6: Helle 2G 15
Linnet Rd. NR8: Cost 2D 12
Linnets, The NR5: New C 6A 14
Lintock Rd. NR3: Norw 4C 16
Linton Cl. NR7: Spro 4G 17
Linton Cres. NR7: Spro 3G 17
Lion & Castle Yd. NR1: Norw 5C 5
Lion Cl. NR5: New C 6F 13
Lion Wood Rd. NR1: Norw 2G 27
Lishman Rd. NR7: Norw 5B 18
Lisle Rd. NR5: Bow 2A 24
Lit. Armes St. NR2: Norw 1H 25
Lit. Bethel Ct. NR2: Norw 5A 5
Lit. Bethel St. NR2: Norw 5A 5 (4C 26)
Lit. Bull Cl. NR3: Norw 1C 4 (2D 26)
Lit. John Rd. NR4: Norw 2B 36
Little La. NR10: H'ford 2G 9
Lit. London St. NR2: Norw 4C 4 (3D 26)
LITTLE MELTON 1F 33
Lit. Melton La. NR4: Coln 6H 23
Lit. Melton Rd.
NR9: Hether, Lit Mel 3D 32
LITTLE PLUMSTEAD 2C 20
Lit. Water La. NR3: Norw 3C 4 (3C 26)
Littlewood NR8: Thor Mar 3H 7
Littlewoods La. NR12: Hov 1D 42
Livingstone St. NR2: Norw 2H 25
Lizard, The NR18: Wym 5E 39
Lloyd Rd. NR1: Norw 2G 27
NR8: Tav 4E 7
Loaning, The NR1: Norw 6E 27
Lobelia Cl. NR18: Wym 2G 39
Lobelia La. NR4: Cring 3D 34
Lobster La. NR2: Norw 4B 4 (3C 26)
Locksley Rd. NR4: Norw 3B 36
Loddon Rd.
NR14: Bix, Fram P, Yelv 2H 37 & 1F 41
Lodge Breck NR8: Dray 6B 8
Lodge Cl. NR5: Norw 4D 24
Lodge Farm Dr. NR6: Old C 6C 10
Lodge La. NR6: Old C 6D 10
Lodge Pl. NR7: Thor And 3B 28
Lodge Rd. NR9: Eas 3A 12
Lodore Av. NR6: Helle 1H 15
Loke, The NR4: Cring 3F 35
NR5: New C 4H 13
NR5: Norw 2F 25
NR13: Blof 1H 31
NR18: Wym 3F 39
Lollards Rd. NR1: Norw 3F 4 (3E 27)
London Rd. NR18: Suton, Wym 6A 38
London St. NR2: Norw 4C 4 (3D 26)
Lone Barn Rd. NR7: Spro 4G 17
Longbow Cl. NR4: Norw 2B 36
Long Dale NR8: Thor Mar 3A 8
Longdell Hills NR5: New C 5H 13
Longe Rd. NR6: Old C 1E 17
Longfields Rd. NR7: Thor And 6D 18
Long John Hill NR1: Norw 1D 36
LONG JOHN'S HILL 1E 37
Longland Cl. NR6: Old C 1D 16
Longlands Dr. NR18: Wym 2B 38
Long La. NR9: Baw 2E 23
(not continuous)
NR13: Stru 5H 31
NR14: Stoke X 4A 40
Longmead NR1: Norw 1D 36
Long Meadow NR13: Brun 4D 30
Long Reach NR13: Brun 3E 31
Long Rd. NR14: Fram E 3C 40
Long Row NR3: Norw 6C 16
Long's Cres. NR13: Rack 1E 19
Longview NR9: Hether 3D 32
Longwater La. NR5: New C 4G 13
NR8: Cost 4G 13
Lonsdale Rd. NR13: Rack 1G 19
Looses Yd. NR3: Norw 2C 4
Lord Nelson Dr. NR5: New C 6F 13
Lord Rosebery M. *NR7: Thor And 3E 29*
(off St Andrews Pk.)
Lorraine Gdns. NR3: Norw 4D 16
Losinga Cres. NR3: Norw 4A 16
Lothian St. NR2: Norw 2B 26
Louis Cl. NR6: Old C 1C 16
Lound Rd. NR4: Norw 4G 25
Lovelace Rd. NR4: Norw 5F 25
Lovelstaithe NR1: Norw 4F 4 (3E 27)
Lovett Cl. NR6: Old C 1E 17
LOW COMMON 6D 22
Lwr. Clarence Rd. NR1: Norw 5F 5 (4E 27)
Lower Cl. NR1: Norw 3E 4 (3E 27)
LOWER EASTON 4A 12
Lwr. Globe La. NR13: Blof 6G 21
Lwr. Goat La. NR2: Norw 4B 4
LOWER HELLESDON 5F 15
Lwr. Spink's La. NR18: Wym 3H 39
Loweswater Gdns. *NR5: Norw 3E 25*
(off Douglas Haig Rd.)
Lowes Yd. NR3: Norw 2C 4
Low Rd. NR4: Kes 4F 35
NR6: Helle, Lwr H 3E 15
NR8: Dray 6B 8
NR9: Eas 4A 12
NR13: Gt P 6F 19 & 6A 20
NR13: Stru 6H 31
Lowry Cole Rd. NR6: Spro 2E 17
Lowther Rd. NR4: Norw 2A 36
Loxwood NR6: Helle 6F 9
Lubbock Cl. NR2: Norw 4G 25
Lucas Ct. NR7: Thor And 6D 18
Lucerne Cl. NR6: Old C 3E 17
Luke Cl. NR5: New C 6A 14
Lupin Cl. NR18: Wym 2G 39
Luscombe Way NR13: Rack 1G 19
Lusher Ri. NR6: Norw 1E 25
Lusher's Loke NR7: Spro 3E 17
Lushington Cl. NR5: Bow 1C 24
Lyhart Rd. NR4: Norw 2A 36
LYNCH GREEN 4D 32
Lynch Grn. NR9: Hether 4C 32
Lyngate Cl. NR9: Hether 5B 32
Lynn Cl. NR7: Thor And 6E 19
Lytton Rd. NR8: Tav 5G 7

M

McCarney Ct. NR6: Helle 2E 15
Mack's La. NR8: Dray, Tav 6G 7
Macmillan Way NR13: Lit P 5B 20
Maddermarket Theatre 4B 4
Maden Cl. NR18: Wym 3C 38
Magdalen Cl. NR3: Norw 1C 4 (1D 26)
Magdalen Rd. NR3: Norw 1D 26
Magdalen St. NR3: Norw 1C 4 (1D 26)
Magistrates' Court
Norwich 2D 4 (2D 26)
Magnay Rd. NR8: Dray 6D 8
Magnolia Cl. NR10: H'ford 1F 9
Magnolia Way NR8: Cost 3D 12
Magpie Cl. NR8: Cost 2D 12
Magpie Rd. NR3: Norw 1C 26
Mahoney Grn. NR13: Rack 1E 19
Maida Vale NR2: Norw 4A 26
Maidens Cl. NR7: Thor And 6F 19
Maid Marian Rd. NR4: Norw 2B 36
Maidstone Rd. NR1: Norw 4D 4 (3D 26)
Malbrook Rd. NR5: Norw 3C 24
Mallard Cl. NR13: Brun 5G 31
Mallory Rd. NR6: Norw 1C 16
Mallow Way NR18: Wym 4E 39
Maltby Ct. NR3: Norw 6E 17
Malten Cl. NR14: Por 5D 40
Malthouse Cl. NR9: Hether 5C 32
Malthouse La. NR2: Norw 6B 5
Malthouse Rd. NR2: Norw 6B 5 (4C 26)
(not continuous)
NR9: Hether 4C 32
Maltsters Yd. NR1: Norw 6D 5 (4D 26)
Malvern Rd. NR1: Norw 3F 27
Malzy Ct. NR3: Norw 1B 4
Manby Rd. NR7: Norw 6H 17
Manchester Pl. NR2: Norw 4B 26
Mancroft St. *NR2: Norw 2B 26*
(off Exeter St.)

52 A-Z Norwich

Mancroft Wlk.—New Costessey

Mancroft Wlk. NR2: Norw 2B 26
Mandela Cl. NR3: Norw 2A 4 (2C 26)
Mandells Ct. NR3: Norw 3C 4
Mangreen La. NR4: Kes, Swar 6A 36
Manor Chase NR8: Tav 5H 7
Manor Cl. NR10: Hor F 1A 10
Manor Cotts. NR13: Blof 1F 31
Mnr. Farm Cl. NR8: Dray 4B 8
Manor Ridge NR13: Blof 1H 31
Manor Rd. NR10: Hor F 1A 10
Mansel Dr. NR6: Old C 4D 16
Mansfield La. NR1: Norw 1D 36
Manthorpe Cl. NR1: Norw 2D 36
Mantle Cl. NR7: Spro 3A 18
Maple Cl. NR18: Wym 2E 39
Maple Dr. NR2: Norw 2G 25
NR8: Tav 3E 7
Marauder Rd. NR6: Norw 1C 16
Mardle St. NR5: Bow 4A 24
Margaret Cl. NR6: Helle 2E 15
Margaret Cres. NR7: Thor And 2C 28
Margaret Paston Av. NR3: Norw 5H 15
Margaret Reeve Cl. NR18: Wym 3E 39
Margaret Rd. NR5: New C 5C 14
Margetson Av. NR7: Thor And 2H 27
Marigold Cl. NR10: H'ford 2F 9
Mariners La. NR1: Norw 7D 5 (5D 26)
Marion Cl. NR18: Wym 3D 38
Marion Rd. NR1: Norw 3F 27
Marion Roberts Ct. NR9: Hether 5C 32
Marionville Rd. NR3: Norw 4D 16
Marjorie Hinde Ct. NR2: Norw 5A 5
Market Av. NR1: Norw 4D 4 (3D 26)
Marketfield La. NR10: Hor F 1C 10
Market La. NR9: Gt Mel, Lit Mel 2A 32
Market Pl. NR2: Norw 4B 4 (4C 26)
NR18: Wym 5D 38
Market St. NR18: Wym 4C 38
Markham Twr. NR3: Norw 5H 15
Mark Lemmon Cl. NR4: Cring 4F 35
MARKSHALL 6D 36
Markshall Farm Rd. NR14: Mark 6B 36
(not continuous)
Markshall La. NR14: Caist E, Mark 6D 36
Marland Rd. NR8: Thor Mar 3G 7
Marlborough Ct. NR1: Norw 4F 27
NR7: Spro 3G 17
Marlborough Ho. NR1: Norw 8A 5
Marlborough Rd. NR3: Norw 1D 26
MARLINGFORD 2A 22
Marlingford Rd. NR9: Baw 2D 22
NR9: Eas, Marl 1A 22
Marlingford Way NR9: Eas 5A 12
Marlow Ct. NR3: Norw 4D 16
Marl Pit La. NR5: Norw 1D 24
Marriott Chase NR8: Thor Mar 4H 7
Marriott Cl. NR2: Norw 2B 26
Marryat Rd. NR7: Norw 6H 17
Marshall Cl. NR5: New C 1C 24
NR10: Spix 2G 11
Marshall Rd. NR3: Norw 4A 16
Marsh Rd. NR12: Hov 2C 42
Marston La. NR4: Norw 3G 35
Marston Moor NR7: Thor And 1E 29
Martin Cl. NR7: Spro 3G 17
Martineau La. NR1: Norw 2E 37
Marvell Grn. NR7: Thor And 6E 19
Marwood Cl. NR18: Wym 5C 38
Mary Chapman Cl. NR7: Thor And 2E 29
Mary Chapman Ct. NR3: Norw 3B 4
Mary Conner Ho. *NR2: Norw 5G 25*
(off Elizabeth Fry Rd.)
Mason Rd. NR6: Norw 4B 16
Massingham Rd. NR3: Norw 6D 16
Matlock Rd. NR1: Norw 4G 27
Maude Gray Ct. *NR2: Norw 3A 4*
(off St Benedicts St.)
Maud St. NR2: Norw 3A 26
Maurice Raes Cl. NR3: Norw 6D 16
Mavish Cl. NR5: Bow 3A 24
Mawkin Cl. NR5: Bow 3A 24
May Cl. NR18: Wym 3C 38
Mayes Cl. NR5: Bow 1C 24
Mayfield Av. NR6: Helle 3A 16
Maze Av. NR8: Cost 2C 12
Meadowbrook Cl. NR1: Norw 6D 26
Meadow Brown Way NR18: Wym 4F 39
Meadow Cl. NR5: New C 5B 14
NR6: Helle 2H 15
NR9: Hether 5C 32
NR14: Tro 1G 37
Meadow Dr. NR12: Hov 3C 42
Meadow Farm Dr. NR4: Cring 5D 34
Meadow Farm La. NR10: Hor F 1B 10
Meadow Gdns. NR6: Spro 3E 17
Meadow La. NR7: Thor And 3C 28
Meadow Rise Av. NR2: Norw 5H 25
Meadow Rise Cl. NR2: Norw 5H 25
Meadow Rise Rd. NR2: Norw 5H 25
Meadow Rd. NR5: New C 5B 14
Meadowsweet NR10: H'ford 2F 9
Meadowsweet Rd. NR18: Wym 4F 39
Meadowvale NR5: New C 4B 14
Meadow Vw. NR13: Brun 3F 31
Meadow Way NR6: Helle 2G 15
NR10: H'ford 2G 9
NR14: Por 5C 40
Meadway NR4: Cring 4D 34
Mecca Bingo
Norwich 5B 16
Medeswell Cl. NR13: Brun 2E 31
Melbourne Cotts. *NR2: Norw 5B 26*
(off Union St.)
Melrose Rd. NR4: Norw 6H 25
Melton Cl. NR18: Wym 2C 38
Melton Ct. NR9: Hether 4C 32
Melton Dr. NR8: Thor Mar 4H 7
Melton Ga. NR18: Wym 3C 38
Melton Rd. NR18: Wym 3C 38
Memorial Way NR7: Thor And 2F 29
Mendham Cl. NR1: Norw 1D 36
Merchants Ct. NR3: Norw 3C 4
Merchants Hill NR2: Norw 6A 5
Merchant Way NR6: Helle 3H 15
Meredith Rd. NR6: Helle 1F 15
Meridian Bus. Pk. NR7: Thor And 4F 29
Meridian Way NR7: Thor And 3F 29
Merlin Av. NR7: Spro 3H 17
Merlin Cl. NR12: Hov 2C 42
Merlin Mews NR7: Spro 3H 17
Merrow Gdns. NR4: Norw 3G 35
Merton Rd. NR2: Norw 2H 25
Metcalf Cl. NR3: Norw 6G 15
Meteor Cl. NR6: Norw 6C 10
Mews, The NR2: Norw 5B 26
Mews Ct. NR13: Blof 1G 31
Middle Rd. NR13: Gt P 6F 19 & 6A 20
Middleton Cl. NR3: Norw 4B 16
Middleton Ct. NR18: Wym 4C 38
Middleton Cres. NR5: New C 5A 14
Middleton's Ct. NR6: Helle 3F 15
Middleton's La. NR6: Helle 3F 15
Middleton St. NR18: Wym 4C 38
Midland St. NR2: Norw 2B 26
Midland Wlk. NR2: Norw 2B 26
Mid-Norfolk Railway
Wymondham Abbey Station 5B 38
MILE CROSS 6H 15
Mile Cross La. NR6: Norw 3A 16
Mile Cross Rd. NR2: Norw 1A 26
NR3: Norw 6A 16
Mile End Cl. NR4: Norw 6H 25
Mile End Rd. NR4: Norw 6H 25
Milestone Cl. NR5: New C 5A 14
Milford Rd. NR2: Norw 4A 26
Mill Cl. NR1: Norw 8C 5 (6D 26)
NR9: Hether 5C 32
NR13: Blof 3G 21
NR14: Por 3B 40
Millcroft NR3: Norw 6D 16
Mill Cft. Cl. NR5: New C 6G 13
Millennium Av. NR6: Helle 2F 15
Millennium Plain NR2: Norw 5B 5
Miller's Breck NR8: Tav 4G 7
Millers La. NR3: Norw 6C 16
Millers Way NR10: H'ford 1G 9
Millfield Cl. NR13: Blof 4G 21
Mill Gdns. NR10: H'ford 1G 9
MILL HILL 6D 16
Mill Hill Rd. NR2: Norw 4A 26
Mill La. NR3: Norw 1D 26
NR4: Kes 5H 35
NR10: H'ford 1G 9
NR10: Hor F 1B 10
NR13: Wit 3B 30
NR14: Bram, Fram P 1G 41
Mill Rd. NR9: Hether 5C 32
NR9: Lit Mel 1D 32
NR13: Blof 3F 21
Mills Cl. NR8: Tav 4F 7
Mill St. NR10: Hor F 2B 10
Millway NR18: Wym 2C 38
Millwrights Way NR3: Norw 5E 17
Milton Cl. NR1: Norw 6D 26
Milverton Rd. NR1: Norw 8E 5 (6E 27)
Minion Cl. NR7: Thor And 1E 29
Mitchell Ct. NR5: Bow 1A 24
Mitre Ct. NR3: Norw 4H 15
Module Bus. Cen. NR6: Norw 2B 16
Mokyll Cft. NR8: Thor Mar 3G 7
Monastery, The NR3: Norw 3C 4 (3D 26)
Monastery Court, The *NR3: Norw 3C 4*
(off The Monastery)
Mons Av. NR1: Norw 1F 27
Montcalm Rd. NR1: Norw 3G 27
Mont Cross NR8: Thor Mar 4G 7
Montgomery Cl. NR5: Bow 2A 24
Montrose Ct. NR7: Thor And 1D 28
Moore Av. NR6: Spro 3E 17
Moorings, The NR3: Norw 2A 4
Moorland Cl. NR7: Norw 5F 17
Moors, The NR8: Thor Mar 3A 8
Morello Cl. NR4: Norw 4F 25
Morgan Ho. NR1: Norw 6D 5
Morgan Way NR5: Bow 1A 24
Morley St. NR3: Norw 1E 4 (1E 27)
Mornington Rd. NR2: Norw 5H 25
Morris Cl. NR5: Bow 1B 24
Morris Dr. NR13: Lit P 5C 20
Morse Av. NR1: Norw 2H 27
Morse Cl. NR13: Brun 4F 31
Morse Rd. NR1: Norw 2H 27
Mosely Ct. NR5: Bow 1H 23
Mossfield Cl. NR1: Norw 1G 27
Mottram Cl. NR5: Norw 3E 25
Motum Rd. NR5: Norw 2D 24
Mountbatten Dr. NR6: Spro 1F 17
Mounteney Cl. NR6: Spro 3E 17
Mountergate NR1: Norw 5E 5 (4E 27)
Mountfield Av. NR6: Helle 3G 15
MOUNT PLEASANT 6H 25
Mt. Pleasant NR2: Norw 5A 26
Mt. Surrey NR18: Wym 2D 38
Mousehold Av. NR3: Norw 1E 27
Mousehold Ho. NR1: Norw 3G 27
Mousehold La. NR7: Norw 4F 17
Mousehold St. NR3: Norw 1E 4 (1E 27)
Mulberry Cl. NR3: Norw 3A 4
NR14: Por 4C 40
Mulberry Ct. NR8: Tav 3E 7
Munnings Rd. NR7: Norw 5A 18
Muriel Kenny Ct. NR9: Hether 5C 32
Muriel Rd. NR2: Norw 5H 25
Murrayfield Rd. NR6: Norw 2A 16
Murrells Ct. NR1: Norw 5D 5
Music Ho. La. NR1: Norw 6E 5 (4E 27)
Musketeer Way NR7: Thor And 2E 29
Musley Ct. NR2: Norw 6A 26
Muspole St. NR3: Norw 2B 4 (2C 26)
Mustard Mill NR1: Norw 8F 5
Myrtle Av. NR8: Cost 4A 14
Myrtle Rd. NR9: Hether 4C 32

N

Naber Furlong NR8: Thor Mar 3G 7
Namco Funscape
Norwich 1A 24
Napier Pl. NR2: Norw 2B 26
Naseby Way NR7: Thor And 2E 29
Nasmith Rd. NR4: Norw 1F 35
Naylor Rd. NR3: Norw 6G 15
Needham Pl. NR1: Norw 7A 5
Nelonde Dr. NR18: Wym 3D 38
Nelson Cl. NR9: Hether 4F 33
NR14: Por 4C 40
Nelson Ct. NR4: Norw 5E 25
Nelson Dr. NR13: Lit P 5C 20
Nelson St. NR2: Norw 2A 26
Nest, The NR1: Norw 4F 4 (3F 27)
Netherconesford *NR1: Norw 5D 5*
(off King St.)
Netherwood Grn. NR1: Norw 1E 37
Neville Cl. NR7: Spro 4E 17
Neville Rd. NR7: Spro 4E 17
Neville St. NR2: Norw 4B 26
Newarch La. NR14: Fram P 1F 41
Newark Cl. NR7: Thor And 2E 29
Newbegin Cl. NR1: Norw 2H 27
Newbegin Rd. NR1: Norw 2G 27
New Botolph St. NR3: Norw 1B 4 (2C 26)
Newbury Way NR7: Thor And 1E 29
Newcastle Cl. NR7: Thor And 1E 29
NEW CATTON 6C 16
NEW COSTESSEY 6A 14

A-Z Norwich 53

Newey's Way—Park & Ride

Newey's Way NR12: Hov . . . 2B **42**
Newfound Dr. NR4: Cring . . . 2D **34**
Newman Rd. NR13: Rack . . . 1E **19**
Newmarket Dr. NR4: Cring . . . 3E **35**
Newmarket Rd. NR1: Norw . . . 8A **5**
NR2: Norw . . . 8A **5** (6A **26**)
NR4: Cring . . . 3C **34**
(not continuous)
Newmarket St. NR2: Norw . . . 5B **26**
New Mills Yd. NR3: Norw . . . 2A **4** (2C **26**)
NEW RACKHEATH . . . 2G **19**
New Rd. NR9: Baw . . . 3E **23**
(not continuous)
NR9: Hether . . . 5B **32**
NEW SPROWSTON . . . 4E **17**
Newton Cl. NR4: Norw . . . 2A **36**
NR14: Tro . . . 1G **37**
Neylond Cres. NR6: Helle . . . 1F **15**
NHS WALK-IN CENTRE
Norwich . . . 3E **29**
Nicholas Ct. *NR3: Norw . . . 6D 16*
(off Magdalen Rd.)
Nicholas M. NR2: Norw . . . 2A **26**
Nicholls Corner NR14: Alp . . . 6H **41**
Nichols Rd. NR14: Alp . . . 5H **41**
Nightingale Cl. NR8: Tav . . . 4E **7**
Nightingale Cotts. NR1: Norw . . . 6E **27**
Nightingale Dr. NR4: Cring . . . 3C **34**
NR8: Tav . . . 4E **7**
Nightingale La. NR3: Norw . . . 1D **4** (1D **26**)
Nightingale M. *NR8: Cost . . . 2E 13*
(off Heron Rd.)
Nile St. NR2: Norw . . . 2A **26**
Nimrod Cl. NR9: Hether . . . 4D **32**
Ninhams Ct. NR2: Norw . . . 5A **5**
Ninham St. NR1: Norw . . . 8D **5** (6D **26**)
Nobel Cres. NR12: Wrox . . . 3A **42**
Noble Cl. NR7: Norw . . . 6A **18**
Noot All. NR5: Bow . . . 2C **24**
Norfolk & Norwich Millennium Library . . . 5B **5**
NORFOLK & NORWICH UNIVERSITY HOSPITAL
. . . 6B **24**
Norfolk Bowling Club . . . 1G **35**
Norfolk Ho. *NR2: Norw . . . 4B 4*
(off Exchange St.)
Norfolk Retail Pk. NR5: New C . . . 5D **12**
Norfolk Rd. NR4: Norw . . . 6D **24**
Norfolk Showground . . . 6D **12**
Norfolk Ski Club . . . 6G **27**
Norfolk St. NR2: Norw . . . 6A **5** (4B **26**)
Norfolk Ter. NR4: Norw . . . 6D **24**
Norgate Rd. NR4: Norw . . . 6F **25**
Norgate Way NR8: Tav . . . 5H **7**
Normandie Twr. NR1: Norw . . . 7E **5**
Norman Dr. NR6: Old C . . . 6D **10**
Norman Recreation Cen. . . . 5A **16**
Norman Rd. NR3: Norw . . . 6D **16**
Normans Bldgs.
NR1: Norw . . . 5D **5** (4D **26**)
Norris Ct. NR3: Norw . . . 3C **4**
Northampton Ct. NR1: Norw . . . 2F **27**
Northcote Rd. NR3: Norw . . . 1D **26**
NORTH EARLHAM . . . 1D **24**
Northfield Cl. NR18: Wym . . . 2C **38**
Northfield Gdns. NR18: Wym . . . 3C **38**
Northfield Loke NR18: Wym . . . 2C **38**
Northfields NR4: Norw . . . 5F **25**
Nth. Gage Cl. NR7: Spro . . . 3H **17**
Northgate NR6: Helle . . . 2G **15**
NR13: Thor E . . . 4E **19**
North Pk. Av. NR4: Norw . . . 6E **25**
North Pk. Dr. NR4: Norw . . . 5G **25**
Northside NR7: Thor And . . . 3E **29**
North St. NR13: Blof . . . 6G **21**
North Ter. NR2: Norw . . . 6B **5**
Northumberland Ct. *NR2: Norw . . . 2A 26*
(off Northumberland St.)
Northumberland St. NR2: Norw . . . 2A **26**
Northview Rd. NR5: New C . . . 6D **14**
Nth. Walsham Rd. NR6: Spro . . . 3E **17**
NR12: Bee A, Crost . . . 3E **17**
Norton Dr. NR4: Norw . . . 2H **35**
Norvic Dr. NR4: Norw . . . 1F **35**
NORWICH . . . 4C **4** (3D **26**)
Norwich Airport Ind. Est. NR6: Norw . . . 1A **16**
(Anson Rd.)
NR6: Norw . . . 6B **10**
(Javelin Rd.)
Norwich Arts Cen. . . . 3A **4**
Norwich Bus. Pk. NR4: Norw . . . 2C **36**
Norwich Cathedral . . . 3D **4** (3E **27**)
Norwich City FC . . . 7F **5** (5F **27**)
Norwich Comn. NR18: Wym . . . 2H **39**
NORWICH COMMUNITY HOSPITAL . . . 2G **25**
Norwich Family Golf Cen. . . . 6B **12**
NORWICH INTERNATIONAL AIRPORT . . . 6A **10**
Norwich Livestock Mkt.
NR4: Norw . . . 4C **36**
Norwich Research Pk. NR4: Coln . . . 5B **24**
Norwich Rd. NR4: Kes . . . 6H **35**
NR5: New C . . . 4C **14**
NR9: Hether . . . 6C **32**
NR10: Hor F . . . 2A **10**
NR12: Sal, Wrox . . . 6A **42**
NR13: Lit P . . . 2H **19** & 2A **20**
NR13: Rack, Sal . . . 1H **19**
NR14: Fram E, Por . . . 1B **40**
NR18: Wym . . . 4D **38**
Norwich St Peter Mancroft Chuch . . . 5B **5**
(off St Peters St)
Norwich Southern By-Pass
NR4: Coln, Cring . . . 1F **23**
NR5: New C . . . 4A **12**
NR9: Baw . . . 1F **23**
NR9: Eas . . . 4A **12**
NR13: Post . . . 6B **28**
NR14: Arm, Caist E, Mark, Tro
. . . 6B **36** & 6B **28**
Norwich Station (Rail) . . . 5F **5** (4E **27**)
Notridge Rd. NR5: Bow . . . 2B **24**
Notykin St. NR5: Bow . . . 1B **24**
Novi Sad Friendship Bridge . . . 7E **5** (5E **27**)
Nurseries Av. NR13: Brun . . . 3G **31**
Nursery Cl. NR6: Helle . . . 2F **15**
Nursery Gdns. NR13: Blof . . . 1H **31**
Nursery La. NR8: Cost . . . 3A **14**
Nutfield Cl. NR4: Norw . . . 2F **35**
Nutwood Cl. NR8: Thor Mar . . . 3G **7**

O

Oak Av. NR7: Thor And . . . 1C **28**
NR14: Por . . . 4C **40**
Oak Cl. NR5: New C . . . 5A **14**
NR9: Hether . . . 4D **32**
Oakcroft Dr. NR14: Fram E . . . 3B **40**
Oakdale Rd. NR13: Brun . . . 4F **31**
Oakfields Cl. NR4: Cring . . . 3F **35**
Oakfields Rd. NR4: Cring . . . 3E **35**
Oak Gro. NR10: H'ford . . . 2G **9**
Oakhill NR13: Brun . . . 4F **31**
Oak Ho. NR5: Bow . . . 1H **23**
Oaklands NR8: Tav . . . 3E **7**
NR14: Fram E . . . 2B **40**
Oaklands Dr. NR4: Cring . . . 2D **34**
Oak La. NR3: Norw . . . 4C **16**
NR6: Old C . . . 4C **16**
Oak Lodge NR7: Norw . . . 4H **27**
Oak Lodge Cotts. NR6: Spro . . . 6G **11**
Oak's La. NR13: Post . . . 4H **29**
Oak St. NR3: Norw . . . 1A **4** (2C **26**)
Oaktree Dr. NR7: Spro . . . 5G **17**
Oak Wood NR13: Blof . . . 2G **31**
Oakwood Dr. NR18: Wym . . . 2F **39**
Oasis Leisure Cen.
Norwich . . . 6D **18**
Oatfield Cl. NR10: H'ford . . . 2F **9**
Octagon Chapel . . . 2C **4**
Octagon Ct. NR3: Norw . . . 2C **4**
Odeon Cinema
Norwich . . . 6F **5** (4E **27**)
Offley Ct. NR5: Bow . . . 1B **24**
Ogden Cl. NR18: Wym . . . 4D **38**
Old Allotment Ct. *NR3: Norw . . . 1E 27*
(off Balfour St.)
Old Bank of England Ct. NR2: Norw . . . 3C **4**
Old Barge Yd. NR1: Norw . . . 6E **5** (4E **27**)
Old Barley Market, The NR2: Norw . . . 4B **4**
OLD CATTON . . . 3D **16**
Old Chapel Way NR7: Thor And . . . 3F **29**
Old Church, The NR1: Norw . . . 4F **4**
Old Church Cl. NR14: Caist E . . . 6E **37**
Old Farm La. NR3: Norw . . . 6A **16**
Old Grove Ct. NR3: Norw . . . 5C **16**
Old Hall Cl. NR14: Tro . . . 1G **37**
Old Hall La. NR10: Spix . . . 2E **11**
Oldhall Rd. NR4: Norw . . . 4B **36**
OLD LAKENHAM . . . 3D **36**
Old Lakenham Hall Dr. NR1: Norw . . . 2D **36**
Old Laundry Ct. NR2: Norw . . . 1A **26**
Old Library M. NR1: Norw . . . 5F **5** (4F **27**)
Old Meeting Ho. All. *NR3: Norw . . . 2C 4*
(off Colegate)
Old Meeting Ho. Yd. *NR3: Norw . . . 2C 4*
(off Colegate)
Old Millers Wharf
NR3: Norw . . . 2D **4** (2D **26**)
Old Mill Rd. NR14: Por . . . 3B **40**
Old Mint Yd. NR3: Norw . . . 2C **4**
Old Norwich Rd. NR10: Hor F . . . 4A **10**
Old Orchard, The NR9: Hether . . . 5E **33**
Old Palace Rd. NR2: Norw . . . 1A **26**
Old Post Office Ct. NR2: Norw . . . 4C **4**
Old Post Office Yd.
NR2: Norw . . . 4C **4** (3D **26**)
Old Rectory Cl. NR7: Thor And . . . 3B **28**
Old School Cl. NR5: Norw . . . 3F **25**
Old School Ct. NR1: Norw . . . 8E **5** (5E **27**)
Old Stoke Rd. NR14: Arm . . . 3E **37**
Old Warren NR8: Thor Mar . . . 3F **7**
Old Watton Rd. NR4: Coln . . . 5B **24**
Olive Cl. NR5: New C . . . 6D **14**
Olive Cres. NR10: H'ford . . . 1F **9**
Olive Rd. NR5: New C . . . 5C **14**
One Post All. NR2: Norw . . . 6B **5**
Onley St. NR2: Norw . . . 5A **26**
Opie St. NR1: Norw . . . 4C **4** (3D **26**)
Orchard Bank NR8: Dray . . . 5H **7**
Orchard Cl. NR7: Norw . . . 1H **27**
NR13: Blof . . . 4F **21**
Orchard Dr. NR6: Helle . . . 4E **15**
Orchard Rd. NR10: Spix . . . 1G **11**
Orchard St. NR2: Norw . . . 2B **26**
Orchard Way NR9: Hether . . . 4D **32**
NR18: Wym . . . 4C **38**
Orford Hill NR1: Norw . . . 5C **5** (4D **26**)
Orford Pl. NR2: Norw . . . 5C **5** (4D **26**)
Orford St. NR1: Norw . . . 5C **5** (4D **26**)
Orford Yd. NR1: Norw . . . 5C **5** (4D **26**)
Oriole Dr. NR4: Cring . . . 3C **34**
Orwell Cl. NR4: Norw . . . 5E **25**
NR18: Wym . . . 3E **39**
Orwell Rd. NR2: Norw . . . 6B **26**
Osbert Cl. NR1: Norw . . . 2D **36**
Osborne Ct. NR2: Norw . . . 6B **26**
Osborne Rd. NR4: Norw . . . 1F **35**
Osprey Cl. NR12: Hov . . . 1C **42**
Osprey Loke NR7: Spro . . . 3H **17**
Ottaway Cl. NR5: New C . . . 4B **14**
Oulton Rd. NR6: Norw . . . 2B **16**
Oval Av. NR5: New C . . . 6D **14**
Oval Rd. NR5: New C . . . 6D **14**
Overbury Rd. NR6: Helle . . . 3H **15**
Overstone Ct. NR6: Old C . . . 2E **17**
Overtons Way NR14: Por . . . 4C **40**
Owen Ct. NR7: Thor And . . . 3F **29**
Oxford St. NR2: Norw . . . 4B **26**
Oxnead Rd. NR3: Norw . . . 5A **16**

P

Paddock, The NR6: Old C . . . 6E **11**
NR14: Tro . . . 1F **37**
Paddocks, The NR6: Old C . . . 1D **16**
Paddock St. NR2: Norw . . . 1B **26**
Padgate NR13: Thor E . . . 4E **19**
Page Cl. NR14: Por . . . 5C **40**
Page Rd. NR3: Norw . . . 6G **15**
NR13: Brun . . . 3E **31**
Pages Cl. NR18: Wym . . . 5C **38**
Paine Rd. NR7: Norw . . . 1A **28**
Palace St. NR3: Norw . . . 3D **4** (3D **26**)
Palgrave Cl. NR8: Tav . . . 4E **7**
Palgrave Ho. NR6: Helle . . . 6F **9**
Palm Cl. NR18: Wym . . . 3C **38**
Palmer Cl. NR3: Norw . . . 5B **16**
Palmer Rd. NR3: Norw . . . 5B **16**
NR13: Rack . . . 1G **19**
Palmers Yd. NR1: Norw . . . 5C **5**
Paper Mill Yd. NR1: Norw . . . 8F **5** (5E **27**)
Papillon Rd. NR18: Wym . . . 4E **39**
Papplewick Cl. NR4: Norw . . . 2B **36**
Paradise Pl. NR1: Norw . . . 6D **5** (4D **26**)
Paragon Pl. NR2: Norw . . . 3B **26**
Parana Cl. NR7: Spro . . . 2H **17**
Parana Ct. NR7: Spro . . . 2H **17**
Parana Rd. NR7: Spro . . . 2H **17**
Park & Ride
Airport . . . 6H **9**
Costessey . . . 6E **13**
Harford . . . 6A **36**
Postwick . . . 4G **29**
Sprowston . . . 1A **18**
Thickthorn . . . 4B **34**

54 A-Z Norwich

Park Cl.—Red Lion St.

Park Cl. NR6: Old C 2D 16
NR9: Hether 5D 32
Park Dr. NR9: Hether 5C 32
Parker Cl. NR13: Brun 3D 30
Parker Rd. NR2: Norw 4A 26
Parkers Cl. NR9: Eas 5B 12
NR18: Wym 2C 38
Park Grn. NR9: Hether 5D 32
Park Ho. NR7: Thor And 3E 29
Park Ho. Ct. *NR3: Norw 4C 16*
(off Catton Gro. Rd.)
Parkland Cres. NR6: Spro 4E 17
Parkland Rd. NR6: Spro 4E 17
Parklands NR8: Cost 3G 13
Park La. NR2: Norw 3A 26
NR13: Blof 5D 20
NR18: Silf, Wym 6D 38
Park Rd. NR10: Spix 3F 11
NR12: Wrox 4A 42
Parkside Dr. NR6: Old C 2D 16
Park Way NR6: Helle 2F 15
Parliament Ct. NR7: Thor And 1E 29
Parmentergate Ct. NR1: Norw 5D 5 (4D 26)
Parmenter Rd. NR4: Norw 6G 25
Parr Rd. NR3: Norw 6H 15
Parsonage Sq. NR2: Norw 4C 4
Parsons Mead NR4: Norw 2G 35
Partridge Way NR6: Norw 3C 16
Paston Ct. NR3: Norw 5A 16
Paston Ho. NR4: Norw 5E 25
Paston Way NR7: Thor And 5B 18
PATCHEY'S CORNER 1F 4 (2E 27)
Patricia Rd. NR1: Norw 6C 26
Patteson Cl. NR4: Cring 4D 34
Patteson Rd. NR3: Norw 1C 26
Pavilion, The NR2: Norw 7A 5 (5C 26)
Pavilion M. NR7: Thor And 3E 29
Paxton Pl. NR2: Norw 5B 26
Peachman Way NR7: Thor And 2F 29
Peacock Chase NR18: Wym 4E 39
Peacock Cl. NR9: Eas 5A 12
Peacock St. NR3: Norw 1C 4 (2D 26)
Peakwell Cl. NR8: Thor Mar 3F 7
Pearcefield NR3: Norw 5D 16
Peck Cl. NR5: Bow 1H 23
Peckover Rd. NR4: Norw 1F 35
Peddars Way NR8: Thor Mar 3G 7
PEDHAM 2H 21
Pedham Rd. NR13: Hemb, Panx 3G 21
Peel M. NR3: Norw 3A 4
Pegg Cl. NR9: Eas 5A 12
Pelargonium Dr. NR18: Wym 1G 39
Pelham Rd. NR3: Norw 6C 16
Pembrey Cl. NR3: Norw 4C 16
Pembroke Rd. NR2: Norw 4A 26
Pendlesham Ri. NR8: Thor Mar 3H 7
Penfold Dr. NR18: Wym 3F 39
Penn Cl. NR8: Tav 5G 7
Penn Gro. NR3: Norw 6B 16
Penn Rd. NR8: Tav 5G 7
Pennycress Dr. NR18: Wym 4F 39
Pennyroyal NR6: Norw 2C 16
Penryn Cl. NR4: Norw 4F 25
Penshurst M. NR4: Norw 2G 35
Percival Cl. NR4: Norw 5F 25
Percy Howes Cl. NR13: Thor E 4E 19
Peregrine Cl. NR7: Spro 3H 17
Peregrine M. NR4: Cring 3C 34
NR7: Spro 3H 17
Peregrine Rd. NR7: Spro 3H 17
Perrings NR18: Wym 2C 38
Peterkin Rd. NR4: Norw 3B 36
Peterson Rd. NR3: Norw 5H 15
Peto Ct. NR5: Norw 2D 24
Pettus Rd. NR4: Norw 6F 25
Petty Spurge Sq. NR18: Wym 4F 39
Petunia Ct. NR18: Wym 1G 39
Peverell Rd. NR5: Bow 2B 24
Phelps Rd. NR7: Thor And 2C 28
Philadelphia La. NR3: Norw 5C 16
Philip Ford Way NR18: Wym 6D 38
Phillipa Ct. NR3: Norw 2C 4
Phillipa Flowerday Plain NR2: Norw 7A 5
Phoenix Yd. *NR3: Norw 1D 4*
(off Leopard Ct.)
Picturehouse Ct. NR5: Norw 1D 24
Pigg La. NR3: Norw 2D 4 (3D 26)
Pigot La. NR14: Fram E, Fram P 3C 40
Pikeman Pl. NR7: Thor And 6F 19
Pilling Pk. Rd. NR1: Norw 2G 27
Pilling Rd. NR7: Thor And 2A 28
Pimpernel Rd. NR10: H'ford 1D 8
Pinder Cl. NR3: Norw 6H 15
Pinder Rd. NR3: Norw 6H 15
Pine Cl. NR4: Norw 6H 25
Pine Ct. NR7: Spro 4A 18
Pinelands Ind. Est. NR10: H'ford 1F 9
Pinelodges, The NR1: Norw 3H 27
Pine Loke NR14: Stoke X 3A 40
Pine Rd. NR7: Thor And 6B 18
Pines, The NR4: Cring 2C 34
Pinetrees Bus. Pk. NR7: Spro 4A 18
Pinetrees Rd. NR7: Spro 4A 18
Pinewood Cl. NR6: Helle 3G 15
Pioneer Rd. NR6: Spro 1F 17
Piper Rd. NR7: Thor And 6B 18
Pippin Grn. NR4: Norw 4F 25
Pishmire Cl. NR5: Bow 3A 24
Pitchford Rd. NR5: Norw 3D 24
Pitt Farm Grn. NR8: R'land 5B 6
Pitt St. NR3: Norw 1B 4 (2C 26)
Plaford Rd. NR7: Norw 5F 17
Plantation, The NR2: Norw 5A 26
Plantation Dr. NR7: Spro 4A 18
Plantation Garden, The 3B 26
Plantation Rd. NR6: Helle 1F 15
NR13: Blof 1G 31
Plantsman Cl. NR2: Norw 6A 26
Plattens Ct. NR12: Wrox 4A 42
Players Way NR6: Old C 1D 16
Playhouse Theatre Norwich 3B 4
Pleasant Cl. NR6: Helle 2E 15
Plough Yd. NR2: Norw 3A 4
PLUMSTEAD GREEN 4A 20
Plumstead Rd. NR1: Norw 2G 27
NR7: Norw 2G 27
NR13: Gt P, Thor E 5E 19
NR13: Panx 1G 21
Plumstead Rd. E. NR7: Norw, Thor And 1H 27
Pochard St. NR8: Cost 2E 13
Pockthorpe Ga. NR3: Norw 1F 4 (2E 27)
Poethlyn Dr. NR8: Cost 2D 12
Pointer Way NR5: Norw 2G 25
Pollywiggle Cl. NR5: Bow 3A 24
Polypin Yd. NR1: Norw 5D 5 (4D 26)
Pond Cl. NR9: Hether 5C 32
Pond La. NR8: Dray 5A 8
Pond Rd. NR10: H'ford 2F 9
Poplar Av. NR4: Norw 2F 35
Poplar Cl. NR5: New C 5H 13
NR10: H'ford 2G 9
Pople St. NR18: Wym 4C 38
Poppy Cl. NR4: Cring 3D 34
Poppyfields NR10: H'ford 2F 9
PORINGLAND 5D 40
Poringland Rd. NR14: Stoke X 4A 40
Porson Rd. NR7: Norw 6H 17
Portersfield Rd. NR2: Norw 4A 26
Porters Loke NR7: Spro 4F 17
Portland St. NR2: Norw 4A 26
Portway Pl. NR2: Norw 2A 26
Portway Sq. NR2: Norw 2B 26
Postle M. NR3: Norw 6H 15
Post Mill Cl. NR7: Spro 4E 17
Postmill Cl. NR18: Wym 4D 38
Post Office Rd. NR13: Lit P 2C 20
POSTWICK 5H 29
Postwick (Park & Ride) 4G 29
Postwick La. NR13: Brun, Wit 4C 30
Pottergate NR2: Norw 4A 4 (3C 26)
Pound La. NR7: Thor And 5D 18
NR13: Blof 2H 31
Poynt Cl. NR18: Wym 3C 38
Press La. NR3: Norw 6B 16
Preston Av. NR18: Wym 6B 38
Preston Cl. NR12: Wrox 5A 42
Pride Way NR7: Thor And 6F 19
Primrose Cres. NR7: Thor And 3D 28
Primrose Pl. NR2: Norw 5A 26
Primrose Rd. NR1: Norw 3F 27
Primrose Way NR10: H'ford 2F 9
Primula Dr. NR4: Norw 4F 25
Prince Andrew's Cl. NR6: Helle 2A 16
Prince Andrew's Rd. NR6: Helle 2A 16
Prince Edward Cl. NR7: Thor And 2C 28
Prince of Wales Rd.
NR1: Norw 4D 4 (3D 26)
Prince Rupert Way NR7: Thor And 5E 19
Princess Beatrice Cl. NR6: Helle 5E 15
Princes St. NR3: Norw 3C 4 (3D 26)
Prior Ct. NR1: Norw 2F 4 (2E 27)
Prior Rd. NR7: Thor And 6D 18
Priors Dr. NR6: Old C 1D 16
Priorswood NR8: Thor Mar 2H 7
Priory, The NR7: Thor And 3E 29
Priory Cl. NR9: Hether 6D 32
NR14: Alp 4H 41
Priory Rd. NR9: Hether 5D 32
Priory Vw. NR1: Norw 8F 5
PRISCILLA BACON CENTRE (HOSPICE) *5H 25*
(within Colman Hospital)
Priscilla Cl. NR5: Norw 3E 25
Proctor Rd. NR6: Old C, Spro 1E 17
Prospect Ter. *NR1: Norw 4F 27*
(off Carrow Rd.)
Providence Pl. NR1: Norw 3F 27
Pudding La. NR2: Norw 5B 5
Pull's Ferry 3F 4 (3E 27)
Pump Ho. Cl. NR8: Cost 3C 12
Puppet Theatre 1D 4 (2D 26)
Purdance Cl. NR5: Bow 1G 23
Purland Rd. NR7: Norw 5A 18
Purtingay Cl. NR4: Norw 2H 35
Pyehurn La. NR10: H'ford 2F 9
Pyehurn M. NR8: Thor Mar 2H 7
Pye's Yd. NR3: Norw 2D 4 (2D 26)
Pym Cl. NR7: Thor And 6F 19
Pyrford Dr. NR4: Norw 2G 35

Q

Quaker La. NR12: Spix 4D 10
Quakers La. NR3: Norw 1B 4
Quarry Rd. NR8: Cost 2D 12
Quayside NR3: Norw 3D 4 (2D 26)
Quebec Cl. NR4: Cring 4D 34
Quebec Rd. NR1: Norw 3F 27
Queen Anne Yd. NR3: Norw 2B 4
Queen Elizabeth Cl. NR3: Norw 2E 4
Queens Cl. NR4: Norw 6H 25
QUEEN'S HILLS 2D 12
Queen's Rd. NR1: Norw 7B 5 (5C 26)
NR9: Hether 4D 32
Queen St. NR2: Norw 4D 4 (3D 26)
NR18: Wym 5D 38
Queensway NR18: Wym 3C 38
Quinton Gurney Ho. NR4: Kes 6G 35

R

Racecourse Rd. NR7: Thor And 6B 18
Rachel Cl. NR5: Norw 4D 24
Rackham Rd. NR3: Norw 5C 16
Rackheath La. NR12: Crost 2H 11
RACKHEATH PARK 1D 18
Radcliffe Rd. NR8: Thor Mar 3H 7
Rafeman Cl. NR5: Bow 2H 23
Raglan St. NR2: Norw 3B 26
Railway Cotts. NR1: Norw 5F 27
Rainsborough Ri. NR7: Thor And 6E 19
Raleigh Ct. NR1: Norw 5D 5
Ramblers, The NR14: Por 1A 40
Rampant Horse St. NR2: Norw 5B 5 (4C 26)
Ramsey Cl. NR4: Norw 6F 25
Randle Grn. NR5: Norw 1D 24
Randolf Rd. NR1: Norw 1D 36
Rangoon Cl. NR7: Spro 2H 17
Ranson Rd. NR1: Norw 4G 27
Ranworth Rd. NR5: Norw 2E 25
NR13: Blof 4H 21
Rattle Row NR18: Wym 4C 38
Raven Cft. NR4: Cring 3C 34
Raven Yd. NR1: Norw 5D 5
Rawley Rd. NR5: Bow 1B 24
Raymond Cl. NR6: Helle 6F 9
Raymond Rd. NR6: Helle 1G 15
Raynham St. NR2: Norw 1B 26
Rayns Cl. NR6: Spro 2E 17
Recorder Rd. NR1: Norw 4E 4 (3E 27)
Recreation Ground Rd. NR7: Spro 3F 17
Recreation Rd. NR2: Norw 4H 25
NR9: Hether 5C 32
Recreation Road Sports Cen. 4H 25
Rectory Ct. NR3: Norw 5C 16
Rectory La. NR9: Lit Mel 1D 32
NR14: Por 5D 40
Red Admiral Cl. NR18: Wym 4F 39
Red Bri. La. NR5: New C 5D 14
Redcliffe Way NR13: Brun 3D 30
Red Cott. Cl. NR3: Norw 5H 15
Redfern Cl. NR7: Norw 6B 18
Redfern Rd. NR7: Norw 6A 18
Red Lion St. NR1: Norw 5C 5 (4D 26)

A-Z Norwich 55

Red Lion Yd.—St Mary's Priory

Red Lion Yd. NR3: Norw . . . 3C 4
Redmayne Vw. NR6: Spro . . . 1F 17
Redpoll Rd. NR8: Cost . . . 1E 13
Red Poll Ter. *NR2: Norw . . . 1D 4*
(off Cow Hill)
Redwell St. NR2: Norw . . . 3C 4 (3D 26)
Redwing Gdns. NR10: Spix . . . 3G 11
Reeder's La. NR14: Alp . . . 6G 41
Reepham Rd. NR6: Helle . . . 1F 15
NR10: Felth, H'ford . . . 1G 7
Reeve's Cnr. NR13: Gt P . . . 3H 19
Regency Ct. NR1: Norw . . . 5F 5
Regency Cres. *NR7: Thor And . . . 3F 29*
(off St Andrews Pk.)
Regina Rd. NR1: Norw . . . 8B 5 (5C 26)
Renson Cl. NR6: Norw . . . 3B 16
Repton Av. NR6: Old C . . . 6C 10
Reve Cres. NR13: Blof . . . 4F 21
Reydon Cl. NR5: Bow . . . 2B 24
Reynolds M. NR18: Wym . . . 3C 38
Rhombus Bus. Pk. NR6: Norw . . . 2A 16
Rhond, The NR12: Hov . . . 2B 42
Rice Way NR7: Spro . . . 5H 17
Richardson Cres. NR9: Hether . . . 4B 32
Richenda Cl. NR5: Norw . . . 4E 25
Richmond Ct. NR7: Thor And . . . 4B 28
RICHMOND HILL . . . 8D 5 (5E 27)
Richmond Rd. NR5: New C . . . 6H 13
Rider Haggard Rd. NR7: Norw . . . 6H 17
Ridgeway, The NR1: Norw . . . 1G 27
Ridings, The NR4: Cring . . . 3E 35
NR14: Por . . . 3B 40
Rigby Cl. NR14: Fram E . . . 3D 40
Rigby's Ct. NR2: Norw . . . 4A 4
Rightup La. NR18: Wym . . . 5E 39
Riley Cl. NR7: Norw . . . 6A 18
Rimer Cl. NR5: Bow . . . 3A 24
Rimington Rd. NR7: Spro . . . 3F 17
Ringers Cl. NR18: Wym . . . 3E 39
RINGLAND . . . 5A 6
Ringland La. NR8: Cost . . . 1C 12
NR8: R'land . . . 4A 6
NR9: Eas . . . 5A 12
Ringland Rd. NR8: R'land, Tav . . . 5B 6
NR9: Eas . . . 3A 12
Ring Rd. NR7: Thor And . . . 2B 28
Ringwood Cl. NR9: Lit Mel . . . 1E 33
Ripley Cl. NR2: Norw . . . 4G 25
Riseway Cl. NR1: Norw . . . 1G 27
Riverdale Ct. NR13: Brun . . . 4F 31
Riverdene M. NR8: Thor Mar . . . 2H 7
River Green Ct. NR7: Thor And . . . 3B 28
River Hgts. NR1: Norw . . . 6E 5
River La. NR3: Norw . . . 1E 4 (2E 27)
Riverside NR1: Norw . . . 5F 5 (4E 27)
Riverside Cl. NR6: Lwr H . . . 5E 15
RIVERSIDE ESTATE . . . 5F 31
Riverside Retail Pk. NR1: Norw . . . 6F 5 (4E 27)
Riverside Rd. NR1: Norw . . . 4F 4 (3E 27)
NR12: Hov . . . 3B 42
Riverside Swimming Cen. . . . 7F 5 (5E 27)
Riverside Wlk. NR1: Norw . . . 6E 5 (4E 27)
NR2: Norw . . . 1A 4 (1B 26)
NR3: Norw . . . 3A 4
Riverway Ct. NR1: Norw . . . 4F 4
Roaches Ct. NR3: Norw . . . 3C 4 (3D 26)
Robberds Way NR5: Bow . . . 1H 23
Robert Cl. NR18: Wym . . . 2D 38
Robert Gybson Way NR2: Norw . . . 3A 4 (3C 26)
NR3: Norw . . . 3C 26
Robert Kett Ct. NR1: Norw . . . 2F 4
Robin Cl. NR8: Cost . . . 2D 12
Robin Ct. NR8: Cost . . . 2D 12
Robin Hood Rd. NR4: Norw . . . 2B 36
Robson Rd. NR5: Norw . . . 3C 24
Rocelin Cl. NR3: Norw . . . 4D 16
Rochester Ct. *NR5: Norw . . . 3D 24*
(off Edgeworth Rd.)
Rockingham Rd. NR5: Norw . . . 3D 24
Rockland Dr. NR7: Thor And . . . 3H 27
Roedich Dr. NR8: Tav . . . 4F 7
Roe Dr. NR5: Norw . . . 3F 25
Rogers Cl. NR5: Norw . . . 2C 24
Rolleston Cl. NR5: Norw . . . 2C 24
Roman Dr. NR13: Brun . . . 3D 30
Romany Rd. NR3: Norw . . . 6E 17
Romany Wlk. NR14: Por . . . 3C 40
Rook Dr. NR8: Thor Mar . . . 3H 7
Ropemakers Row NR3: Norw . . . 6B 16
Ropes Wlk. NR13: Blof . . . 1G 31
Rosa Cl. NR10: Spix . . . 3H 11
Rosalie Cl. NR6: Helle . . . 3A 16
Rosary Rd. NR1: Norw . . . 3F 4 (3F 27)
Roseacre Cl. NR2: Norw . . . 1B 36
Rose Av. NR1: Norw . . . 5D 5 (4D 26)
NR8: Cost . . . 3D 12
Rosebay Cl. NR6: Norw . . . 2C 16
Rosebery Av. NR14: Por . . . 4D 40
Rosebery Ct. NR7: Thor And . . . 3E 29
Rosebery Rd. NR3: Norw . . . 6C 16
NR13: Gt P . . . 1A 30
Rose Cotts. NR10: Hor F . . . 2B 10
Rosedale Cres. NR1: Norw . . . 4F 27
Rosefields NR13: Brun . . . 3G 31
Rose La. NR1: Norw . . . 5D 5 (4D 26)
Rosemary La. NR3: Norw . . . 2B 4 (2C 26)
Rosemary Rd. NR7: Spro . . . 3G 17
NR13: Blof . . . 3F 21
Rosetta Rd. NR10: Spix . . . 2H 11
Rose Valley NR2: Norw . . . 4A 26
Roseville Cl. NR1: Norw . . . 4G 27
Rose Wlk. NR13: Brun . . . 4E 31
Rose Yd. NR3: Norw . . . 1B 4 (2C 26)
Rosslare NR4: Norw . . . 2H 35
Rossons Rd. NR8: Tav . . . 4F 7
Rostwold Way NR3: Norw . . . 5C 16
Rotary Ct. NR6: Lwr H . . . 5F 15
Rotary Ho. NR1: Norw . . . 8F 5
Rothbury Cl. NR18: Wym . . . 4C 38
Rothbury Rd. NR18: Wym . . . 4D 38
Rouen Rd. NR1: Norw . . . 5D 5 (4D 26)
Roundhead Ct. NR7: Thor And . . . 2E 29
Round Ho. Way NR4: Cring . . . 2C 34
Roundtree Cl. NR7: Spro . . . 5G 17
Roundtree Cl. Ind. Est. NR7: Spro . . . 5G 17
Roundtree Trad. Est. NR7: Spro . . . 5G 17
Roundtree Way NR7: Spro . . . 5G 17
Roundway Down NR7: Thor And . . . 1E 29
Round Well Rd. NR5: New C . . . 6G 13
Rowan Cl. NR18: Wym . . . 3F 39
Rowan Ct. NR5: New C . . . 6A 14
NR7: Spro . . . 4A 18
Rowan Gdns. NR9: Hether . . . 5C 32
Rowington Rd. NR1: Norw . . . 8B 5 (5C 26)
Rowland Ct. NR1: Norw . . . 8D 5 (5D 26)
Rowton Heath NR7: Thor And . . . 1E 29
Roxley Cl. NR7: Thor And . . . 4C 28
Royal Arc. NR2: Norw . . . 5C 5
Royal Arch Ct. *NR2: Norw . . . 3B 26*
(off Earlham Rd.)
Royalist Dr. NR7: Thor And . . . 2E 29
Royal Norwich Golf Course . . . 4F 15
Royal Oak Ct. NR1: Norw . . . 6D 5
Rufus St. NR8: Cost . . . 2D 12
Rugge Dr. NR4: Norw . . . 1F 35
Rumsey Wells Pl. NR2: Norw . . . 4B 4
Runcton Cl. NR5: Norw . . . 2C 24
Runnel, The NR5: Bow . . . 3A 24
Runnymede *NR3: Norw . . . 2C 4*
(off Golden Dog La.)
Rupert St. NR2: Norw . . . 5B 26
(not continuous)
Rushmore Cl. NR7: Spro . . . 2F 17
Rushmore Rd. NR7: Spro . . . 2F 17
Ruskin Rd. NR4: Norw . . . 5F 25
NR5: New C . . . 6C 14
Russell Av. NR7: Spro . . . 4F 17
NR10: Spix . . . 2G 11
Russell St. NR2: Norw . . . 2B 26
Russell Ter. NR14: Tro . . . 1G 37
Russell Way NR18: Wym . . . 5D 38
Russet Gro. NR4: Norw . . . 4F 25
Rustens Mnr. Rd. NR18: Wym . . . 3D 38
Rutland St. NR2: Norw . . . 5B 26
Rydal Cl. NR5: Norw . . . 3D 24
Rye Av. NR3: Norw . . . 4A 16
Rye Cl. NR3: Norw . . . 5A 16
Ryrie Ct. NR4: Norw . . . 1G 35

S

Sadler Rd. NR6: Helle . . . 6G 9
Saffron Sq. NR3: Norw . . . 4B 16
Sainsbury Cen. for Visual Arts . . . 6C 24
St Alban's Rd. NR1: Norw . . . 6C 26
St Andrews & Blackfriars Halls . . . 3C 4
St Andrews Av. NR7: Thor And . . . 3D 28
St Andrews Bus. Pk. NR7: Thor And . . . 3E 29
St Andrews Cl. NR7: Thor And . . . 3D 28
NR13: Blof . . . 2G 31
NR14: Fram E . . . 3E 41
NR14: Por . . . 4D 40
St Andrews Dr. NR4: Norw . . . 3F 35
St Andrews Hall Plain
NR3: Norw . . . 3C 4 (3D 26)
St Andrews Hill NR2: Norw . . . 4C 4 (3D 26)
St Andrews Pk. NR7: Thor And . . . 3E 29
St Andrew's Rd. NR6: Helle . . . 1E 15
St Andrews Sq. NR7: Thor And . . . 3E 29
St Andrews St. NR2: Norw . . . 4C 4 (3C 26)
St Andrew's Way NR13: Blof . . . 2G 31
St Annes Cl. NR13: Brun . . . 5H 31
St Annes Rd. NR14: Fram E . . . 4D 40
St Ann La. NR1: Norw . . . 6E 5 (4E 27)
St Augustines Ga. *NR3: Norw . . . 1C 26*
(off Waterloo Rd.)
St Augustines St. NR3: Norw . . . 1B 4 (1C 26)
St Barnabas Ct. *NR2: Norw . . . 2B 26*
(off Orchard St.)
St Bartholomews Cl. NR2: Norw . . . 1A 26
St Benedicts St. NR2: Norw . . . 3A 4 (3B 26)
St Catherine's Rd. NR7: Thor And . . . 1C 28
St Clements All. NR3: Norw . . . 2C 4
St Clements Hill NR3: Norw . . . 6D 16
St Clements Way NR13: Brun . . . 3E 31
St Crispins Rd. NR3: Norw . . . 1A 4 (2C 26)
St Davids Dr. NR13: Thor E . . . 4E 19
St David's Rd. NR9: Hether . . . 6C 32
St Edmund Cl. NR14: Caist E . . . 2A 40
St Edmund's Cl. NR6: Lwr H . . . 6F 15
NR8: Cost . . . 2A 14
St Edmund's Ri. NR8: Tav . . . 5F 7
St Edmund's Rd. NR8: Tav . . . 4F 7
St Edmunds Wharf NR3: Norw . . . 2D 4
St Ethelberts Gate . . . 3D 4
St Faith Crematorium
NR10: Hor F . . . 1A 10
St Faiths La. NR1: Norw . . . 4D 4 (3D 26)
St Faiths Rd. NR6: Old C . . . 2C 16
St George Loke *NR7: Spro . . . 3E 17*
(off School La.)
St Georges All. NR3: Norw . . . 2B 4
St Georges St. NR3: Norw . . . 2B 4 (2C 26)
St Giles St. NR2: Norw . . . 4A 4 (3C 26)
St Giles Ter. NR2: Norw . . . 4A 4
St Gregory's All. NR2: Norw . . . 4B 4
St Gregory's Bk. All. *NR2: Norw . . . 4B 4*
(off Charing Cross)
St Gregory's Cen. for the Arts . . . 4B 4
St Helena Way NR10: H'ford . . . 1F 9
St Helen's Sq. NR1: Norw . . . 2E 4 (2E 27)
St James Cl. NR3: Norw . . . 1F 4 (2E 27)
St James Ct. NR3: Norw . . . 1D 4 (2D 26)
St James Ho. NR3: Norw . . . 1F 4
St James Mdw. NR3: Norw . . . 2F 4 (2E 27)
St James Mill NR3: Norw . . . 1D 4 (2D 26)
St John Maddermarket
NR2: Norw . . . 4B 4 (3C 26)
St John's All. NR2: Norw . . . 4B 4
St John's Cl. NR1: Norw . . . 1D 36
NR9: Hether . . . 6C 32
St John St. NR1: Norw . . . 5D 5 (4E 27)
St Julians All. NR1: Norw . . . 6D 5 (4D 26)
St Laurence Av. NR13: Brun . . . 3D 30
St Lawrence Cl. NR2: Norw . . . 4A 4
St Lawrence Dr. NR4: Cring . . . 2D 34
St Lawrence La. NR2: Norw . . . 4B 4 (3C 26)
St Lawrence Lit. Steps *NR2: Norw . . . 3A 4*
(off Westwick St.)
St Lawrence Steps *NR2: Norw . . . 3B 4*
(off Westwick St.)
St Leonards Cl. NR18: Wym . . . 2D 38
St Leonards Rd. NR1: Norw . . . 4F 4 (3F 27)
St Leonard's Ter. NR1: Norw . . . 3F 27
St Margarets All. NR2: Norw . . . 3A 4
St Margarets Cl. NR8: Thor Mar . . . 2A 8
St Margarets Dr. NR7: Spro . . . 2G 17
St Margarets Gdns. NR12: Hov . . . 2C 42
St Margarets St. NR2: Norw . . . 3A 4 (3C 26)
St Martin at Bale Ct. NR1: Norw . . . 5D 5
St Martin at Palace Plain
NR3: Norw . . . 2D 4 (2D 26)
St Martins at Oak Wall La.
NR3: Norw . . . 1A 4
St Martin's Cl. NR3: Norw . . . 1A 4 (1C 26)
St Martin's La. NR3: Norw . . . 2A 4 (2C 26)
St Martin's Rd. NR3: Norw . . . 1A 4 (1C 26)
St Mary's All. NR3: Norw . . . 2B 4
St Marys Cl. NR10: Hor F . . . 2B 10
NR12: Wrox . . . 3A 42
NR13: Gt P . . . 6A 20
NR14: Alp . . . 4H 41
St Marys Gro. NR7: Spro . . . 2H 17
St Mary's Plain NR3: Norw . . . 2B 4 (2C 26)
St Mary's Priory (remains) . . . 6F 27

56 A-Z Norwich

St Marys Rd.—Station Cotts.

St Marys Rd. NR3: Norw . . . 1C 26
NR14: Por . . . 4D 40
St Matthews Rd. NR1: Norw . . . 4F 4 (3E 27)
St Michael at Pleas NR3: Norw . . . 3D 4
St Michaels Way NR13: Brun . . . 5H 31
St Michael Ter. *NR1: Norw* . . . *3F 27*
(off St Leonards Rd.)
St Mildreds Rd. NR5: Norw . . . 3C 24
St Miles All. NR3: Norw . . . 2B 4
St Olaves Rd. NR3: Norw . . . 1D 26
St Paul's Cl. NR6: Helle . . . 2H 15
NR10: H'ford . . . 1G 9
St Paul's Sq. NR3: Norw . . . 1D 4
St Peter Hungate Church . . . 3C 4
St Peters Cl. NR4: Cring . . . 3E 35
St Peters Ct. NR1: Norw . . . 5D 5 (4D 26)
St Peters Dr. NR9: Eas . . . 5A 12
St Peters St. NR2: Norw . . . 4B 4 (3C 26)
St Peter's Way NR10: Spix . . . 2G 11
St Philips Rd. NR2: Norw . . . 3A 26
St Saviours All. NR3: Norw . . . 1C 4
St Saviours La. NR3: Norw . . . 2C 4 (2D 26)
Saints Ct. NR1: Norw . . . 6C 5
St Simon Cl. NR8: Cost . . . 2D 12
St Simon Ct. NR3: Norw . . . 3D 4
St Stephens Arc. NR2: Norw . . . 6B 5
St Stephens Plain *NR1: Norw* . . . *6C 5*
(off St Stephens St.)
St Stephens Rd. NR1: Norw . . . 8A 5 (5C 26)
St Stephens Sq. NR1: Norw . . . 7A 5 (5C 26)
St Stephens St. NR1: Norw . . . 6B 5 (4C 26)
St Swithins All. NR2: Norw . . . 3A 4
St Swithins Rd. NR2: Norw . . . 3A 4 (3C 26)
St Swithins Ter. *NR2: Norw* . . . *3A 4*
(off St Benedicts St.)
St Thomas Dr. NR18: Wym . . . 6D 38
St Thomas Rd. NR2: Norw . . . 3H 25
St Vedast St. NR1: Norw . . . 4E 4 (3E 27)
St Walstans Cl. NR5: New C . . . 6G 13
NR8: Tav . . . 5G 7
St Walstan's Rd. NR8: Tav . . . 4G 7
St Williams Way NR7: Thor And . . . 1H 27
Saker Cl. NR7: Thor And . . . 1E 29
Sale Rd. NR7: Norw . . . 5A 18
Salhouse Rd. NR7: Norw, Rack, Spro . . . 5H 17
NR12: Wrox . . . 5A 42
NR13: Lit P . . . 1C 20
NR13: Rack . . . 1G 19
Salhouse Rd. Ind. Est. NR7: Spro . . . 5H 17
Salisbury Rd. NR1: Norw . . . 4G 27
Salter Av. NR4: Norw . . . 4F 25
Salvia Cl. NR18: Wym . . . 2G 39
Salvin Ct. NR5: Norw . . . 2C 24
Samson & Hercules Ho. NR3: Norw . . . 3D 4
Samson Rd. NR6: Helle . . . 3G 15
Samuel Rd. NR1: Norw . . . 1G 27
Sandhole La. NR13: Lit P . . . 2B 20
Sandholme Cl. NR1: Norw . . . 1G 27
Sandringham Ct. NR2: Norw . . . 8A 5
Sandringham Rd. NR2: Norw . . . 3A 26
Sandy La. NR1: Norw . . . 3D 36
NR4: Norw . . . 2C 36
NR8: Tav . . . 5F 7
NR9: Eas . . . 2A 12
NR10: H'ford . . . 1F 9
Santolina Cl. NR5: New C . . . 6C 14
Sapphire Way NR6: Norw . . . 2A 16
Saracen Rd. NR6: Helle . . . 1G 15
Sarah West Cl. NR2: Norw . . . 7A 5 (5B 26)
Sarah Williman Cl. NR5: Norw . . . 4D 24
Saunders Ct. NR1: Norw . . . 3F 27
Savery Cl. NR5: Norw . . . 3C 24
Sawmill Cl. NR18: Wym . . . 3C 38
Sawyers Cl. NR5: New C . . . 6H 13
Saxonfields NR14: Por . . . 5C 40
Sayers St. NR2: Norw . . . 2B 26
(not continuous)
Scarlet Rd. NR4: Norw . . . 2C 36
Scarnell Rd. NR5: Norw . . . 3E 25
Sceptre Cl. NR6: Helle . . . 4H 15
Scholars Ct. NR3: Norw . . . 2B 4
School Av. NR7: Thor And . . . 3C 28
School Cl. NR13: Blof . . . 1G 31
School La. NR2: Norw . . . 4C 4
NR7: Spro . . . 3E 17
NR7: Thor And . . . 3A 28
NR9: Lit Mel . . . 1F 33
NR10: H'ford . . . 2G 9
School Rd. NR8: Dray . . . 4A 8
NR13: Blof, Lit P . . . 4C 20
School Ter. NR14: Tro . . . 1G 37
Scoles Grn. NR1: Norw . . . 5D 5
Scotch Hill Rd. NR8: Tav . . . 4E 7
Scott Rd. NR1: Norw . . . 4G 27
Scott's Ct. NR1: Norw . . . 6C 5
Scott's Yd. NR1: Norw . . . 7D 5
Seabrook Ct. NR5: Bow . . . 2B 24
Seaforth Dr. NR8: Tav . . . 5H 7
Seaman Twr. NR3: Norw . . . 5H 15
Seates, The NR8: Thor Mar . . . 3G 7
Sebald Ho. *NR2: Norw* . . . *5G 25*
(off Kinghorn Rd.)
Sedman Wlk. *NR5: Bow* . . . *1B 24*
(off Rawley Rd.)
Sego Vale NR8: Tav . . . 5H 7
Seppings Way NR13: Thor E . . . 4E 19
Seton Rd. NR8: Tav . . . 4H 7
Sewell Barn Theatre . . . 5D 16
Sewell Ct. NR6: Old C . . . 6E 11
Sewell Pk. Sports Centre, The . . . 5D 16
Sewell Rd. NR3: Norw . . . 5D 16
Shack La. NR13: Blof . . . 1E 31
Shakespeare Way NR8: Tav . . . 5G 7
Sheep Mdw. Cl. NR5: New C . . . 6A 14
Sheffield Rd. NR18: Wym . . . 2D 38
Shelley Dr. NR8: Tav . . . 5G 7
Shepherd Cl. NR5: Norw . . . 4E 25
Shepherds Cl. NR10: H'ford . . . 2F 9
Shepherd Way NR8: Thor Mar . . . 3H 7
Sherbourne Pl. NR1: Norw . . . 7E 5 (4E 27)
Sheridan Cl. NR8: Dray . . . 5A 8
Sherwell Rd. NR6: Helle . . . 1F 15
Sherwood Rd. NR4: Norw . . . 2B 36
Sherwyn Ho. *NR3: Norw* . . . *2B 4*
(off Winterton La.)
Shibleys Ct. NR2: Norw . . . 4A 4
Shillgate Way NR8: Thor Mar . . . 3E 7
Shillito Rd. NR13: Blof . . . 1H 31
Shipfield NR3: Norw . . . 5E 17
Shipstone Rd. NR3: Norw . . . 1C 26
Shire Hall - Royal Norfolk Regimental Mus. . . . 5C 5 (3D 26)
Shires, The NR8: Thor Mar . . . 3A 8
Shooters Cl. NR8: Tav . . . 4G 7
Shop La. NR9: Hether . . . 4F 33
Shorncliffe Av. NR3: Norw . . . 6A 16
Shorncliffe Cl. NR3: Norw . . . 6B 16
Shotesham Rd. NR14: Por . . . 6B 40
Showmens Guild Caravan Site
NR3: Norw . . . 5E 17
Shrublands, The *NR2: Norw* . . . *3A 26*
(off West Pottergate)
NR10: H'ford . . . 1F 9
Sidell Cl. NR4: Cring . . . 4D 34
Sidestrand NR1: Norw . . . 7F 5
Sidings, The NR1: Norw . . . 4H 27
Sidney Rd. NR8: Cost . . . 3A 14
Sienna M. NR1: Norw . . . 2G 27
Sigismund Rd. NR1: Norw . . . 8B 5 (6C 26)
Silfield Av. NR18: Wym . . . 6E 39
Silfield Rd. NR18: Silf, Wym . . . 6D 38
Silkfields NR3: Norw . . . 2A 4 (2C 26)
Silver Birch Ct. NR3: Norw . . . 5H 15
Silver Haven *NR3: Norw* . . . *1E 27*
(off Mousehold Av.)
Silver Rd. NR3: Norw . . . 1E 4 (6E 17)
Silver St. NR3: Norw . . . 1D 4 (1D 26)
Silvo Rd. NR8: Cost . . . 1D 12
Singer Ct. *NR3: Norw* . . . *2C 4*
(off Calvert St.)
Sir Alfred Munning's Rd. NR5: New C . . . 4D 12
NR8: Cost . . . 4D 12
Sir Thomas Beevor Cl. NR18: Wym . . . 3D 38
Siskin Cl. NR8: Cost . . . 2D 12
Sixteen Acre Rd. NR2: Norw . . . 4G 25
Skedge Way NR13: Blof . . . 4E 21
Skelton Rd. NR7: Norw . . . 1H 27
Skinners La. NR12: Wrox . . . 5A 42
Skipping Block Row NR18: Wym . . . 1H 39
Skippon Way NR7: Thor And . . . 6E 19
Skoner Rd. NR5: Bow . . . 1C 24
Skye Cl. NR5: Bow . . . 1B 24
Slade La. NR14: Fram P, Yelv . . . 1G 41
Sleaford Grn. NR3: Norw . . . 5B 16
Smeat St. NR5: Bow . . . 2C 24
Smee La. NR13: Gt P . . . 1G 29 & 1A 30
Smithdale Rd. NR5: New C . . . 6C 14
Smithfield Rd. NR1: Norw . . . 6D 26
Smithson Cl. NR18: Wym . . . 3D 38
Smock Mill Loke NR18: Wym . . . 3C 38
Snowberry Cl. NR8: Tav . . . 3E 7
Snowdrop St. NR18: Wym . . . 2G 39
Softley Dr. NR4: Cring . . . 1D 34
Solario Rd. NR8: Cost . . . 2D 12
Sole Cl. NR10: H'ford . . . 2G 9
Soleme Rd. NR3: Norw . . . 5A 16
Somerleyton Gdns. NR2: Norw . . . 4B 26
Somerleyton St. NR2: Norw . . . 4B 26
Somerset Way NR8: Tav . . . 4D 6
Sonya Ter. NR1: Norw . . . 2G 27
Sorrel Ho. NR5: Bow . . . 1B 24
Sotherton Rd. NR4: Norw . . . 6G 25
Southalls Way NR3: Norw . . . 6E 17
South Av. NR7: Thor And . . . 4B 28
South Cft. NR9: Hether . . . 5C 32
Southerwood NR6: Norw . . . 2C 16
Southfield La. NR13: W'wick . . . 1E 21
Sth. Gage Cl. NR7: Spro . . . 3A 18
Southgate La. NR1: Norw . . . 8E 5 (5E 27)
South Hill Cl. NR7: Thor And . . . 1C 28
South Hill Rd. NR7: Thor And . . . 6C 18
South Pk. Av. NR4: Norw . . . 6F 25
South Wlk. NR13: Thor E . . . 5E 19
Southwell Rd. NR1: Norw . . . 8B 5 (5C 26)
NR10: Hor F . . . 2H 9
Sth. Wood Dr. NR14: Caist E . . . 2A 40
Sovereign Ho. NR3: Norw . . . 1C 4
Sovereign Way NR3: Norw . . . 1C 4
Sparhawk Av. NR7: Spro . . . 3H 17
Sparhawk Cl. NR7: Spro . . . 3H 17
Spar Rd. NR6: Norw . . . 2B 16
Speedwell Rd. NR18: Wym . . . 4E 39
Speedwell Way NR5: Bow . . . 4A 24
Speke St. NR2: Norw . . . 2H 25
Spelman Rd. NR2: Norw . . . 5H 25
Spencer Cl. NR13: Lit P . . . 2C 20
Spencer Rd. NR6: Norw . . . 2B 16
Spencer St. NR3: Norw . . . 1D 26
Spindle Cl. NR18: Wym . . . 4E 39
Spindle Rd. NR6: Norw . . . 3C 16
Spink's La. NR18: Wym . . . 2G 39
Spinney Cl. NR7: Thor And . . . 1C 28
Spinney Rd. NR7: Thor And . . . 1B 28
SPIRE NORWICH HOSPITAL . . . 4B 24
Spitalfields NR1: Norw . . . 2F 27
Spitfire Rd. NR6: Norw . . . 1B 16
SPIXWORTH . . . 2H 11
Spixworth Rd. NR6: Old C . . . 4D 16
NR10: Hor F . . . 2A 10
Sportspark
(Sports Cen. and Swimming Pool) . . . 5E 25
Springbank NR1: Norw . . . 1D 36
Springdale Cres. NR13: Brun . . . 3D 30
Springdale Rd. NR13: Brun . . . 3D 30
Springfield Rd. NR7: Norw . . . 5A 18
NR8: Tav . . . 4F 7
Springfields NR14: Por . . . 4C 40
Springwood NR8: Thor Mar . . . 4H 7
SPROWSTON . . . 3G 17
Sprowston (Park & Ride) . . . 1A 18
Sprowston Manor Golf Course . . . 1B 18
Sprowston Retail Pk. NR7: Spro . . . 5H 17
Sprowston Rd. NR3: Norw . . . 6D 16
Spruce Cres. NR14: Por . . . 4C 40
Spur Ind. Est. NR18: Wym . . . 4D 38
Spur La. NR14: Fram E . . . 2C 40
Spynke Rd. NR3: Norw . . . 4A 16
Square, The NR4: Norw . . . 5D 24
NR8: Thor Mar . . . 3H 7
Squire's Haven NR1: Norw . . . 4F 27
Stacy Rd. NR3: Norw . . . 1D 26
Stafford Av. NR5: New C . . . 6A 14
Stafford St. NR2: Norw . . . 3H 25
Staithe La. NR13: Brun . . . 4F 31
Staitheway Rd. NR12: Wrox . . . 3B 42
Stalham Rd. NR12: Hov . . . 2C 42
Stalham Rd. Ind. Est. NR12: Hov . . . 1D 42
Stamp Office Yd. NR3: Norw . . . 3C 4
Standley Ct. NR18: Wym . . . 4C 38
Stanfield Rd. NR18: Wym . . . 5G 39
Stanford Ct. NR5: Norw . . . 3F 25
Stanford Cres. NR13: Lit P . . . 2C 20
Stanley Av. NR7: Norw . . . 4H 27
Stanleys La. NR18: Wym . . . 6D 38
Stanmore Cl. NR7: Thor And . . . 3B 28
Stanmore Rd. NR7: Thor And . . . 3B 28
Stannard Pl. NR3: Norw . . . 2C 4
Stannard Rd. NR4: Norw . . . 4G 25
Stan Petersen Cl. NR1: Norw . . . 3F 27
Starling Ct. NR8: Cost . . . 2D 12
Starling Rd. NR3: Norw . . . 1C 26
Starling St. NR8: Cost . . . 2E 13
Statham Cl. NR4: Norw . . . 1A 36
Station App. NR1: Norw . . . 5F 5 (4E 27)
NR18: Wym . . . 6D 38
Station Cotts. NR9: Hether . . . 6H 33

A-Z Norwich 57